Our Catholic Faith

A Summary of Basic Beliefs

Rev. Msgr. John F. Barry, P.A.

Oscar

Sadlier

A Division of William H. Sadlier, Inc.

Nihil Obstat
Karen Wilhelmy, C.S.J.
Censor Deputatus

Imprimatur
✠ His Eminence
Cardinal Roger M. Mahony
Archbishop of Los Angeles
December 3, 2008

The *Nihil Obstat* and *Imprimatur* are official declarations that the work contains nothing contrary to Faith and Morals. It is not implied, thereby that those granting the *Nihil Obstat* and *Imprimatur* agree with the contents, statements or opinions expressed.

The Subcommittee on the Catechism, United States Conference of Catholic Bishops, has found this catechetical text, copyright 2009, to be in conformity with the *Catechism of the Catholic Church.*

Acknowledgments
Excerpts from the English translation of *The Roman Missal,* © 2010, International Committee on English in the Liturgy, Inc. All rights reserved.

Scripture excerpts from the *New American Bible* with *Revised New Testament and Psalms.* Copyright © 1991, 1986, 1970. Confraternity of Christian Doctrine, Inc., Washington, D.C. Used with permission. All rights reserved. No portion of the *New American Bible* may be reprinted without permission in writing from the copyright holder.

Excerpts from the English translation of *Rite of Baptism for Children* © 1969, International Committee on English in the Liturgy, Inc. (ICEL); excerpts from the English translation of *Rite of Penance* © 1974, ICEL; excerpts from the English translation of *Rite of Confirmation (Second Edition)* © 1975, ICEL; excerpts from the English translation of *A Book of Prayers* © 1982, ICEL; excerpts from the English translation of *Order of Christian Funerals* © 1985, ICEL; excerpts from the English translation of *Book of Blessings* © 1988, ICEL. All rights reserved.

William H. Sadlier, Inc.
9 Pine Street
New York, NY 10005-4700

ISBN: 978-0-8215-1264-7
8 9 10 WEBC 16 15 14

Catechetical and Liturgical Consultants

Vilma Angulo
Director of Religious Education
All Saints Catholic Church
Sunrise, FL

John Benson
Catechist
All Saints Catholic Church
Sunrise, FL

Carol Craven
Director of Religious Education
St. Paul the Apostle Catholic Church
New Middletown, OH

Carole Eipers, D. Min.
Vice President, Executive Director of Catechetics
William H. Sadlier, Inc.

Mary Larsen
Director of Religious Education
St. Mary's Church
South Amboy, NJ

Reverend Nicholas Shori
Pastor
St. Paul the Apostle Catholic Church
New Middletown, OH

Official Theological Consultant

Most Reverend Edward K. Braxton, Ph.D., S.T.D.
Bishop of Belleville, IL

Sadlier Consulting Team

Michaela Burke Barry
Ken Doran
Dulce M. Jiménez-Abreu
Saundra Kennedy, Ed.D.
William M. Ippolito
Ida Iris Miranda
Victor Venezuela

Writing/Development Team

Rosemary K. Calicchio
Vice President, Publications

Blake Bergen
Editorial Director

Melissa D. Gibbons
Director of Research and Development

Mary Ann Trevaskiss
Supervising Editor

Maureen Gallo
Senior Editor

Allison Johnston
Editor

Publishing Operations Team

Deborah Jones
Vice President, Publishing Operations

Vince Gallo
Creative Director

Francesca O'Malley
Associate Art Director

Jim Saylor
Photography Manager

Design Staff
Debrah Kaiser
Andrea Brown

Production Staff
Tresse DeLorenzo
Jovito Pagkalinawan
Diane Ali
Maria Jiménez

Contents

A Wonderful World

God has filled our world
with so many wonderful gifts.

Which of God's wonderful gifts are your favorites?

Describe these gifts in words or through art.

baleball

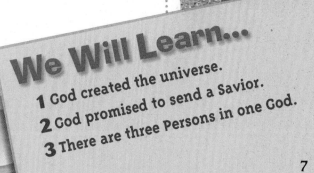

We Will Learn...

1 God created the universe.

2 God promised to send a Savior.

3 There are three Persons in one God.

1 God created the universe.

The **Bible** is the book about God's love for us and about our call to live as God's people. God is the author of the Bible since he guided the writers to record the things he wanted to share with us. We call the Bible the Word of God.

As we read the first book of the Bible, Genesis, we learn that everything in the universe was created by God. In the story of Creation, we read that after God created the sky, the bodies of water, the land, and the animals, God created human beings. God loved human beings so much he created us in his image and likeness. "God created man in his image; . . . /male and female he created them." (Genesis 1:27)

God gave the first human beings, whom we call Adam and Eve, the ability to love, to think and wonder, to ask questions and look for answers, and to make choices. God's plan for human beings was that they be happy with him forever.

God gave the first humans the whole of Creation to enjoy and protect. God wanted people to love and to be happy and to share in his goodness and beauty. We can read the whole story of Creation in Genesis 1:1—2:4 and Genesis 2:4–25.

When we see the beauty of Creation, we realize a loving God has given us everything. We should take time to thank him. We can do this by respecting each person because she or he is made in the image and likeness of God. We can also do this by taking care of the world—God's gift to us—so that we can share its goodness with all people.

In what ways can you show respect for others this week?

In what ways can you care for God's gifts of Creation?

Do You Know?

God alone created the world. He created each person in his image and likeness. Each person is a unity of body and soul. The soul is the invisible and the spiritual reality that makes each of us human. The soul is immortal, which means it will never die. At death the soul is separated from the body. But the soul will be reunited with the body when Christ comes in glory at the end of time.

2 God promised to send a Savior.

One of God's greatest gifts to humans is the gift of free will. The first humans were free to choose either to do good or evil. God would not force them to do anything. God trusted them to act out of love for him rather than selfishness. In God's plan, humans would live in peace and harmony. They would never be sick or die.

But in Genesis, we learn how evil entered the world. We read that tempted by the devil, Adam and Eve chose not to use their freedom wisely. They chose to act selfishly and to turn away from the loving God who had created them. When they chose to turn away from God, they committed the first sin, called **Original Sin**. This sin weakened human nature and brought ignorance, suffering, and death into the world.

From then on all human beings have been born with Original Sin.

Even though the first humans sinned, God still loved them. He promised that he would not turn away from his people. God promised that he would send a Savior—someone who would save them from sin. In God's plan, through the power of the Holy Spirit, God the Father would send his only Son to save all people from sin.

Why do you think free will is one of God's greatest gifts?

9

There are three Persons in one God.

God the Father, God the Son, and God the Holy Spirit are three Persons in one God. We call the three Persons in one God: God the Father, God the Son, and God the Holy Spirit, the **Blessed Trinity**. The Blessed Trinity is a mystery of faith. It is a belief that we will not fully understand until we are sharing life forever with God in Heaven. The Blessed Trinity is the central belief of our faith and of our life of faith.

One way to show our belief in the Blessed Trinity is to pray the Sign of the Cross.

When will you pray the Sign of the Cross this week?

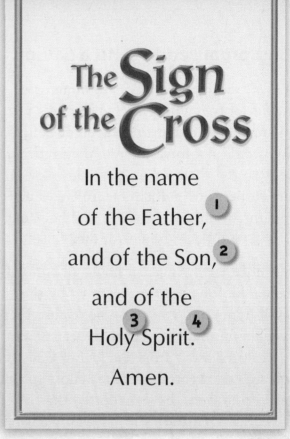

The Sign of the Cross

In the name

of the Father, 1

and of the Son, 2

and of the

Holy Spirit. 3 4

Amen.

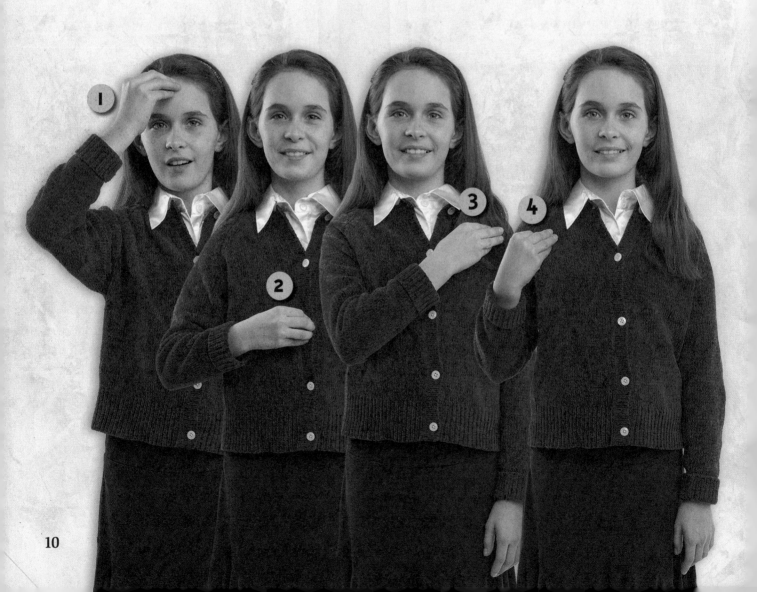

Complete the following sentences.

1. God created people in his _____ *imd* and likeness.

2. The _____ *bible* is the book about God's love for us and our call to live as God's people.

3. God promised to send us a _____ *Savior* to save us from sin.

4. We call the three Persons in one God: God the Father, God the Son, and God the Holy Spirit, the _____ *trinity*.

Discuss the following.

5. What did God want people to do with the world he had created?

6. What are the effects of Original Sin?

7. What was God's promise to Adam and Eve after they sinned?

Faith Words

Bible (page 8)

Original Sin (page 9)

Blessed Trinity (page 10)

With My Family

Sharing Our Faith

 1 God created the universe.

 2 God promised to send a Savior.

 3 There are three Persons in one God.

PRAYING TOGETHER

Praise the Blessed Trinity often this week by praying:

Glory to the Father, and to the Son,
    and to the Holy Spirit:
as it was in the beginning,
    is now, and will be for ever. Amen.

Living Our Faith

This week remind your family members that God gave us the world to enjoy and protect. Together list ways you can protect the environment. Choose one or two ways from your list to work on together this week.

_____

_____

_____

_____

_____

_____

_____

A Day for Good News

Last Tuesday Mr. Diaz picked up Victor and Rosa after school. They ran to the car. They could not wait to share their great news.

Victor told his dad, "Our principal announced the prize winners of the school read-a-thon. Guess what! Mrs. Fielding announced my name as the second prize winner. I was so surprised!"

Mr. Diaz said, "I'm so proud of you, Victor. What is your prize?"

Victor answered,

" A New Car
_____
_____ ."

(fill in your answer)

Then Rosa said, "I have good news, too. My friend Emily's cat had kittens last Sunday. Emily brought in some pictures. The kittens are so cute! Emily's mom said that I could have one of the kittens. I told Emily that I would have to talk to you and Mom first. If you say yes, I'm going to name the kitten

Tail
_____ ."

(fill in your answer)

Mr. Diaz said, "Now I have good news to tell you. Grandpa sent me a text message today. He and Grandma are coming to visit. They are going to drive from their new home in South Carolina. They'll be here in time for the family picnic next Saturday."

Victor and Rosa cheered. Then Victor said, "We have a lot to tell Mom when she comes home tonight."

Mr. Diaz said, "You're right, Victor. I think we should celebrate."

He continued, "Let's go out for dinner. On the way to the restaurant we can take turns telling Mom our good news."

Rosa said, "And maybe Mom will have good news to tell us, too!"

. . .

What good news have you heard recently?

Who shared the good news with you?

With whom did you share the news?

We Will Learn...

1 Jesus Christ is true God and true man.

2 Jesus shares the Good News of God's love.

3 Jesus teaches about the Kingdom of God.

13

1 Jesus Christ is true God and true man.

The truth that God the Son, the second Person of the Blessed Trinity, became man is called the **Incarnation**. We learn about this mystery of our faith in the Bible.

In the Gospel of Luke, we read that one day the angel Gabriel gave a message to a young Jewish woman named Mary. Gabriel told Mary that God wanted her to be the mother of his Son. The angel also told Mary that she was to name the child *Jesus*, which means "God saves."

Do You Know?

Angels are creatures created by God as pure spirits. They do not have physical bodies. Angels serve God as his messengers. They serve God in his saving plan for us and constantly give him praise.

Mary told the angel that she did not fully understand how this would happen. The angel answered, "The holy Spirit will come upon you, and the power of the Most High will overshadow you. Therefore the child to be born will be called holy, the Son of God" (Luke 1:35).

Mary agreed to be the Mother of God's Son. She gave birth to a son and called him Jesus. Jesus Christ is truly the Son of God and Mary's Son. Jesus Christ is both divine and human. **Divine** is a word we use to describe God.

Jesus Christ is divine; he is Lord. He did things only God can do. He is also human; he is like us in all things, except he is without sin.

What do we mean by the Incarnation?

14

2 Jesus shares the Good News of God's love.

When Jesus was about thirty years old, he began his work among the people. Jesus was to share the love of God with all people and to save all people from sin. So Jesus' mission was to spread the Good News of God's love.

And all of Jesus' words and actions—from his miracles and prayers to his Crucifixion and Resurrection—were carried out through the guidance of the Holy Spirit. Jesus' whole life was a continual teaching.

Through his words and actions Jesus taught people to know and love God. He

- fed the hungry
- cured the sick
- forgave sinners
- was a friend to those who were sick or in need
- showed people how to love God
- taught people to love others as God loves them.

Jesus told the people that God loves, forgives, and cares for all of us. No one is left out. He called people to follow him and share his mission. Many people accepted Jesus' invitation. Those who followed him were his **disciples**.

Jesus chose twelve of his disciples to lead the community of his followers. These twelve men whom Jesus chose to share in his mission in a special way are the **Apostles**.

This week how can you show that you want to follow Jesus as his disciple?

Jesus teaches about the Kingdom of God.

Crowds of people followed Jesus everywhere he went. They wanted to hear him teach. Jesus often spoke about the Kingdom of God. He told them, "The kingdom of God is at hand" (Mark 1:15).

The Kingdom of God is not a place you can find on a map. The **Kingdom of God** is the power of God's love active in our lives and in our world. The Kingdom of God was made present through Jesus' words and actions.

Jesus taught us about God's Kingdom in special stories called parables. In one parable Jesus said that the Kingdom of God was like a great treasure that people would want above all things. (See Matthew 13:44.)

In another parable Jesus said that the Kingdom of God was like a mustard seed, a tiny seed that grows into a very large plant. (See Matthew 13:31–32.)

Jesus taught that the way to live for God's Kingdom is by turning away from sin and doing what God asks us to do. All people are invited to become a part of the Kingdom and to spread God's love in the world. All people are invited to become faithful followers of Jesus.

The Kingdom of God will not be complete until Jesus returns in glory at the end of time. So each day we work and live for God's Kingdom as we look forward to being with God forever in Heaven.

How do we live for the Kingdom of God?

Write the letter of the answer that best defines each term.

1. _____ D Apostles

2. _____ c parable

3. _____ b divine

4. _____ a disciples

a. those who followed Jesus

b. a word used to describe God

c. a special story Jesus told

d. the twelve men whom Jesus chose to share in his mission in a special way

Discuss the following.

5. What is the Incarnation?

6. What is the Kingdom of God?

Faith Words

Incarnation (page 14)

divine (page 14)

disciples (page 15)

Apostles (page 15)

Kingdom of God (page 16)

With My Family

Sharing Our Faith

 1 Jesus Christ is true God and true man.

2 Jesus shares the Good News of God's love.

 3 Jesus teaches about the Kingdom of God.

PRAYING TOGETHER

In the Lord's Prayer we pray for the fulfillment of God's Kingdom.

Our Father, who art in heaven,
hallowed be thy name;
thy kingdom come;
thy will be done on earth
as it is in heaven.
Give us this day our daily bread;
and forgive us our trespasses
as we forgive those who trespass against us;
and lead us not into temptation,
but deliver us from evil. Amen.

Living Our Faith

This week with your family, read and discuss one or two of Jesus' parables about the Kingdom of God. (See Matthew 13.) Decide which parable is most meaningful for you. Then write about or draw a picture of one or two ways you can help spread the Kingdom of God.

Sign of Hope and Love

Last month Alexa Federov's home was partly destroyed by a storm. So she and her parents went to stay at her Aunt Anna's house. Every day Alexa's parents traveled back to their home, and worked to clean up and repair the house.

One morning when Alexa woke up, she heard noises outside. She got up and went to see what was happening. It was Aunt Anna carefully hammering broken dishes on a table in the driveway. Alexa was confused and asked, "What are you doing, Aunt Anna?"

Aunt Anna explained, "Your mom and dad brought back a box of these broken dishes.

Your mom treasured these dishes because the set was a wedding gift from your grandparents. Your mom was upset when she saw the dishes broken and scattered. She couldn't bring herself to throw away the pieces."

Alexa asked, "Then why are you breaking the dishes into smaller pieces?"

"I'm going to use the pieces to make a special gift for your mom. I'm going to make a mosaic cross. Would you like to help me, Alexa?" Aunt Anna asked.

Alexa wanted to help, so she and Aunt Anna worked on the mosaic all morning. While they were working, Alexa asked, "Why are we making a cross?"

Aunt Anna said, "For me a cross is a sign of hope. I think about Jesus' love for us. I remember that he died on the cross and rose from the dead for us. I also remember that he promised to be with us always. When your house is repaired, your parents can hang the cross where all of you will see it often. As you look at it, you can think about Jesus' love.

You can remember that Jesus is with you in happy, peaceful times as well as in troubled, stormy times."

• • •

What do you think Alexa's parents will say when they see the cross?

What do you think about when you see a cross?

We Will Learn...

1 Jesus gave us the Eucharist at the Last Supper.

2 Jesus died on the cross to save us from sin.

3 Jesus rose from the dead and brought us new life.

Jesus gave us the Eucharist at the Last Supper.

Every year Jewish people gather to celebrate the Feast of Passover. In the time of Jesus, many gathered in Jerusalem for the feast. They praised and worshiped God in the Temple there.

Jesus and his disciples went to Jerusalem on the Sunday before Jesus died. They stayed in the city all week, and Jesus taught outside the Temple every day.

On the night before Jesus died, he and his disciples gathered to celebrate the Passover meal. At the meal Jesus gave the disciples a special way to remember him and to be with him. Here is what Jesus said and did at the meal. "While they were eating, he took bread, said the blessing, broke it, and gave it to them, and said, 'Take it; this is my body.'

Then he took a cup, gave thanks, and gave it to them, and they all drank from it. He said to them, 'This is my blood.'"
(Mark 14:22–24)

Since this was the last meal Jesus shared with his disciples before he died, we call this meal the **Last Supper**. At the Last Supper Jesus gave himself to the disciples in the bread and wine which became his Body and Blood.

At the Last Supper Jesus gave us the gift of the Eucharist. The Eucharist is the sacrament of the Body and Blood of Jesus Christ. Jesus is really present under the appearances of bread and wine. This true presence of Jesus Christ in the Eucharist is called the **Real Presence**.

On the night before Jesus died, what did he do for his disciples?

2 Jesus died on the cross to save us from sin.

Some powerful leaders did not believe that Jesus was the Son of God. They plotted against him. After the Last Supper, Jesus went to pray in a garden with some of the Apostles. While they were there, the leaders had Jesus arrested.

The next morning Jesus was sentenced to die. The soldiers forced Jesus to carry a heavy cross to Calvary, a hill outside Jerusalem. There Jesus was crucified—that is, nailed to a cross. Yet, even as he was dying, Jesus forgave those who had crucified him. He prayed: "Father, forgive them, they know not what they do" (Luke 23:34).

Do You Know?

On the Feast of Passover the Jewish people remember and celebrate the wondrous way that God saved their ancestors from slavery and death in Egypt. God "passed over" the houses of his people, protecting them from the suffering that came to the Egyptians—the death of every first-born son. God then saved Moses and the Israelites by helping them to cross the Red Sea and flee Egypt. God made a covenant, an agreement, with Moses as he had made an everlasting covenant with Noah and all living beings after the flood and as he had with Abraham and his descendants. By the covenant God made with Moses and the Israelites, God would be their God, protecting and providing for them, and they would be his people.

Through Jesus Christ's Death and Resurrection, a new covenant was made between God and his people. Through this new covenant we are saved. We can share in God's life again.

Jesus' mother Mary, other women disciples, and the Apostle John stayed by Jesus as he suffered and died on the cross. Many of Jesus' disciples hid because they were afraid that they, too, would be arrested.

Christ of Saint John of the Cross, Salvador Dali, 1951

After Jesus died, his body was taken down from the cross and laid in a tomb. A great stone was rolled in front of it. Then, filled with sadness, the disciples left to return to the places where they were staying.

Why was Jesus sentenced to die?

3 Jesus rose from the dead and brought us new life.

Early on the Sunday morning after Jesus died, some women disciples went to the tomb to anoint Jesus' body. As the women neared the tomb, they saw that the stone in front of it had been rolled back. The women thought someone had stolen Jesus' body.

But then the women saw two men in dazzling garments. The men said, "Why do you seek the living one among the dead? He is not here, but he has been raised" (Luke 24:5–6).

The women ran to tell the Apostles that Jesus had risen from the dead just as he had told them he would do. The mystery of Jesus Christ rising from the dead is the **Resurrection**.

Through his Death and Resurrection, Jesus Christ saved us from the power of sin and death. Jesus is our Savior. **Savior** is a title given to Jesus because he died and rose from the dead to save us. Jesus promised that his faithful followers would also share in his Resurrection and have eternal life. Through Jesus Christ, our risen Savior, we have new life—we share in God's own life now and have the hope of living with God forever.

Each year we celebrate the Feast of the Resurrection of Jesus Christ on Easter Sunday.

How do you think Jesus' disciples felt when they heard that he had risen from the dead?

Write *True* or *False* next to the following sentences. On a separate piece of paper, change the false sentences to make them true.

1. _____ Jesus and his disciples went to Egypt to celebrate the Feast of Passover.

2. _____ Jesus gave himself to us in the Eucharist on the night before he died.

3. _____ Most of Jesus' disciples stayed with Jesus as he died on the cross.

4. _____ The women disciples shared the news about Jesus rising.

Discuss the following.

5. Why were Jesus and his disciples in Jerusalem during the week before he died?

6. Why did some powerful leaders have Jesus arrested and sentenced to death?

7. What did Jesus do for us through his Death and Resurrection?

Faith Words

Last Supper (page 20)

Real Presence (page 20)

Resurrection (page 22)

Savior (page 22)

With My Family

Sharing Our Faith

 Jesus gave us the Eucharist at the Last Supper.

 Jesus died on the cross to save us from sin.

 Jesus rose from the dead and brought us new life.

PRAYING TOGETHER

At Mass after the bread and wine are changed into the Body and Blood of Christ, the priest invites us to proclaim our faith. Here are two of the acclamations we pray:

Save us, Savior of the world,
for by your Cross and Resurrection
you have set us free.

We proclaim your Death, O Lord,
and profess your Resurrection
until you come again.

Pray these acclamations often during the week. Remember all that Jesus has done for us by his Death on the cross and his Resurrection.

Living Our Faith

In this chapter you learned that as Jesus was dying on the cross, he forgave those who crucified him. With your family talk about the importance of forgiveness. If there are people who have hurt you or treated you unfairly, forgive them by talking with them or by forgiving them in your heart. Ask forgiveness of any person whom you have hurt.

DIVINE REVELATION God loves us so much that he told us about himself. He revealed himself to us. To *reveal* means "to make known." Divine Revelation is God's making himself known to us through his mighty deeds and by his interactions with his people throughout time.

God made himself known gradually over time. Revelation began with the creation of the first human beings and their descendants. It continued through the time of the ancient Israelites and the Jewish people. God's Revelation is full and complete in his only Son, Jesus Christ. The Church is guided by the Holy Spirit to understand God's Revelation. God's Revelation is handed down through the Bible and Tradition.

THE BIBLE AND TRADITION The Bible, also called Sacred Scripture, is the written record of God's Revelation. The Bible has a divine author, God, and many human writers. The Holy Spirit guided these writers as they wrote. The special guidance that the Holy Spirit gave to the human writers is called *Divine Inspiration*. It guaranteed that they wrote without any error God's saving truth. For that reason, God is the true author of the Bible.

The word *bible* means "books." The Bible is made up of seventy-three separate books. It is divided into two parts: the Old Testament and the New Testament. They contain Salvation history.

The Old Testament contains forty-six books. In the Old Testament we learn about God's relationship with the people of Israel.

The New Testament contains twenty-seven books. In the New Testament we learn about Jesus Christ, his first followers, and the beginning of the Church. The four Gospels of the New Testament contain the message and key events in the life of Jesus Christ. Because of this, the Gospels hold a central place in the New Testament.

Tradition is the Revelation of the Good News of Jesus Christ as lived out in the Church, past and present. Tradition includes teachings and practices handed on orally from the time of Jesus and his Apostles. It includes the creeds, or statements, of Christian beliefs.

Write *True* or *False* next to the following sentences. On a separate sheet of paper, change the false sentences to make them true.

1. _____ We call the Bible the Word of God.

2. _____ The Blessed Trinity is the central belief of our faith.

3. _____ No one stayed with Jesus as he died on the cross.

4. _____ Human beings are born with Original Sin.

5. _____ The disciples were the twelve men whom Jesus chose to share in his mission in a special way.

Put the following biblical events in the order in which they happened. Use numbers 1–5.

6. God promised to send a Savior. _____

7. At the Last Supper, Jesus gave us the gift of himself in the Eucharist. _____

8. Jesus shared the Good News of God's love. _____

9. Jesus was crucified, died, and rose from the dead. _____

10. Jesus, God's own Son, became man. _____

Write your responses on a separate sheet of paper.

11. Name two ways Jesus spread the Good News of God's love.

12. What is the Kingdom of God?

13. What is the Incarnation?

14. Who are the three Persons of the Blessed Trinity?

15. What did Jesus do for us through his Death and Resurrection?

A Family Helper

After dinner Brian was doing his homework. His older brother Kevin walked into the family room. He asked, "Brian, what do you have for homework tonight?"

Brian answered, "Right now I'm completing a writing assignment. I'm writing about a person I admire, and I'm giving a few reasons for my choice."

Kevin asked, "Who are you writing about?"

"Surprise, Kevin! I'm writing about you," Brian answered.

Kevin pointed to himself and said, "Me? Why are you writing about me?"

Brian explained, "You do a lot for me, Kevin. You really came to the rescue when Dad told us we were moving to Springfield. Do you remember how upset I was? I ran outside and sat on the back steps. You were upset, too, but you came outside and talked to me. You helped calm me down, especially when you told me to think about moving as an adventure. You told me we'd have new places to explore and new friends to meet."

"That wasn't a big deal," Kevin said.

"It was a big deal to me," Brian answered. "Then after we moved you watched out for me. That first week of school was the hardest for me, but you waited for me every day after school.

You stayed with me at the first Nature Scout meeting we went to, and you introduced me to some of the scouts you knew from school."

Kevin said, "I only did what I thought an older brother should do. Now let's see what you think about your older brother when I win a game of chess. Whoever loses helps with the dishes every night this week!"

How did Kevin help Brian?

Who are your family helpers?

How do they help your family?

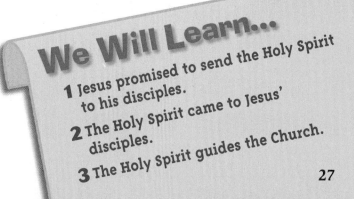

We Will Learn...

1 Jesus promised to send the Holy Spirit to his disciples.

2 The Holy Spirit came to Jesus' disciples.

3 The Holy Spirit guides the Church.

1 Jesus promised to send the Holy Spirit to his disciples.

Jesus knew that after his work on earth was complete his disciples would need help in living as he had asked them to live. Jesus promised that the Holy Spirit would come to them and strengthen them. The Holy Spirit would help the disciples to remember all that Jesus had taught them.

After Jesus' Death and Resurrection, he appeared to his disciples several times. Then forty days after he rose from the dead, Jesus called his Apostles to a mountain in Galilee. He told them that he wanted them to continue his mission to bring the Good News of God's love to the world. Jesus said, "Go, therefore, and make disciples of all nations, baptizing them in the name of the Father, and of the Son, and of the holy Spirit, teaching them to observe all that I have commanded you. And behold, I am with you always, until the end of the age" (Matthew 28:19–20).

After Jesus gave this mission to the Apostles, he returned to his Father in Heaven. Jesus' return in all his glory to his Father in Heaven is called the **Ascension**.

After Jesus' Ascension, the Apostles returned to Jerusalem. There with the other disciples they prayed as they waited for the Holy Spirit to come to them.

Why did Jesus promise his disciples that the Holy Spirit would come to them?

What was the mission Jesus gave to his Apostles?

2 The Holy Spirit came to Jesus' disciples.

Early on Sunday morning, fifty days after Jesus rose from the dead, Jesus' disciples were together in Jerusalem. They were praying and waiting for the Holy Spirit. As they prayed, something amazing happened. "And suddenly there came from the sky a noise like a strong driving wind, and it filled the entire house in which they were. Then there appeared to them tongues as of fire, which parted and came to rest on each one of them. And they were all filled with the holy Spirit and began to speak in different tongues, as the Spirit enabled them to proclaim." (Acts of the Apostles 2:2–4)

On this day Peter and the disciples were no longer afraid to speak about Jesus and his teachings. They left the house and went out into the streets. Crowds of people were in Jerusalem to celebrate a great Jewish feast. Peter spoke to these people, telling them to be baptized and thus to receive the Gift of the Holy Spirit. "Those who accepted his message were baptized, and about three thousand persons were added that day." (Acts of the Apostles 2:41)

The day the Holy Spirit came upon Jesus' disciples is called **Pentecost**. It was on this day that the Church began. The **Church** is the community of people who are baptized and follow Jesus Christ. On Pentecost and throughout the whole year we remember that the Holy Spirit is with the Church always.

How did the Holy Spirit help Peter and the disciples on Pentecost?

3 The Holy Spirit guides the Church.

Jesus had chosen the Apostle Peter as the head of the Church. On Pentecost, the Holy Spirit filled Peter and the other disciples of Jesus with courage and love. With the help of the Holy Spirit, they began to share the Good News of Jesus Christ with everyone they met. They showed others how to live according to the teachings of Jesus by:

- sharing what they had with the poor
- taking care of those who were sick or disabled
- gathering together to pray
- celebrating the Eucharist in Jesus' memory
- celebrating the presence of the risen Christ among them.

More and more people asked to be baptized. They wanted to follow Jesus and to be part of his community—to be members of the Church. The Apostle Peter described the Church as "God's people" (1 Peter 2:10) —the people baptized as God's children, brothers and sisters of Jesus.

With the guidance of the Holy Spirit, the Church spread throughout the world. The Holy Spirit helped the Church, the People of God, to love God and one another.

The Holy Spirit helped the members of the Church to share the Good News of Jesus Christ with everyone in the world. And the Holy Spirit continues to help and guide the Church today in the interpretation of Sacred Scripture and in the official teachings of the Church, which we call Tradition. Through Tradition the Holy Spirit teaches us to pray.

How did the Holy Spirit help the early Christians?

Do You Know?

The early Christians needed to understand the special relationship Jesus Christ had with his community, the Church. Saint Paul, an early Christian who traveled to different countries sharing the Good News of Jesus Christ, explained that the Church is the Body of Christ (1 Corinthians 12:27). Christ is the Head (Colossians 1:18), but everyone in the Church is an important part of the Body of Christ.

Each member of the Church receives the Holy Spirit at Baptism. Saint Paul also taught that the Church is the Temple of the Holy Spirit (1 Corinthians 3:16). So the Holy Spirit is at the heart of the Church's life and growth, uniting us through our love for and belief in Jesus Christ.

Complete the following sentences.

1–2. The Ascension is

_____

_____

_____

_____

3–4. The Church is

the church is a

comunity

_____

_____

_____

Discuss the following.

5. Before he returned to Heaven, what did Jesus ask his disciples to do?

6. Describe briefly what happened on Pentecost.

7. How did the early Christians share their love for God and one another?

Faith Words

Ascension (page 28)

Pentecost (page 29)

Church (page 29)

With My Family

Sharing Our Faith

1 Jesus promised to send the Holy Spirit to his disciples.

2 The Holy Spirit came to Jesus' disciples.

3 The Holy Spirit guides the Church.

PRAYING TOGETHER

This prayer to the Holy Spirit is a traditional prayer of the Church.

Come, Holy Spirit, fill the hearts
   of your faithful.
And kindle in them the fire
   of your love.

Send forth your Spirit and they
   shall be created.
And you will renew the face
   of the earth. Amen.

• ·· Living Our Faith · ·•

The Holy Spirit helped the Apostles and the early Christians to share God's love with others. The way in which Jesus' followers lived helped others to experience the power of his love. This week think about the people who help you experience the power of Jesus' love. Decide on one way to thank each person.

Name	Way of Thanks

5

Imagine that talk-show hosts are interviewing you. Write your response to each of the following questions on the lines provided.

Discuss these questions with family members and friends.

Why are leaders necessary?

becouse

.

What are some words that describe good leaders?

thunkful

.

Who are some good leaders you know?

my mom

_____ .

How can you develop
good leadership skills?

_____

_____ .

We Will Learn...

1 The pope and bishops are the successors of the Apostles.

2 The Church is one, holy, catholic, and apostolic.

3 Catholics worship and serve together.

1 The pope and bishops are the successors of the Apostles.

After the coming of the Holy Spirit on Pentecost, the Apostles traveled from place to place teaching what Jesus had taught them. In each local community the Apostles baptized people as Jesus had commanded them. The members of these communities looked to Peter and the other Apostles as their leaders.

The Apostles eventually chose local leaders to serve these communities. The Apostles laid their hands on the heads of those they had chosen and asked the Holy Spirit to strengthen and guide these new leaders in their work. In this way the Apostles handed on what Christ had given to them: the authority to carry on his mission.

As time passed, the leaders who succeeded, or took the place of, the Apostles were called *bishops*. **Bishops** are the successors of the Apostles and continue to lead the Church. Each local area of the Church is called a **diocese** and is led by a bishop.

The **pope** is the bishop of the diocese of Rome, Italy. He continues the leadership of the Apostle Peter, having a God-given responsibility to care for the souls of all members of the Church. Together with all the bishops, the pope leads and guides the whole Catholic Church. Under the leadership of the pope and bishops, the Church continues the work of Jesus Christ each and every day. Each of us is united with the pope and bishops in living out our faith.

Who is our present pope?

Who is the bishop of your diocese?

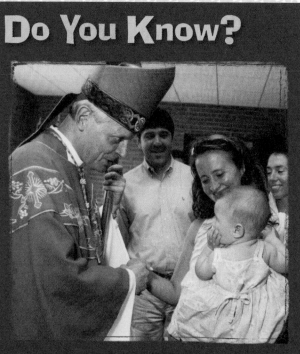

Do You Know?

The bishops continue the mission of the Apostles in three important ways:

- They *teach*. The bishops are the chief teachers of the Church. They help the members of the Church know, understand, and live out the teachings of Jesus Christ.

- They *lead*. The bishops are the chief leaders and pastors of the Church. They lead their people and oversee the work of their dioceses.

- They *sanctify*. The word *sanctify* means "to make holy." Through their prayer, preaching, and celebration of the sacraments, the bishops help all the members of the Church to live Christian lives and to grow in holiness.

2 The Church is one, holy, catholic, and apostolic.

In the Catholic Church, the Church of Christ is truly present although elements of goodness and truth can be found outside of her. The Catholic Church has four very special qualities or characteristics. The Church is one, holy, catholic, and apostolic. These four characteristics that describe the Church are called the **Marks of the Church**.

The Church is *one*. The Church is one because all of her members believe in the one Lord, Jesus Christ. We share the same Baptism and are guided and united by the Holy Spirit. Under the leadership of the pope and bishops, we gather together to celebrate the sacraments and to live and work together as one community called together by God.

The Church is *holy*. God alone is all good and holy. But he shared his holiness with all people by sending his Son, Jesus Christ to us. As members of the Church, baptized into the Body of Christ, we, too, through the power of the Holy Spirit, share in God's life which makes us holy.

As members of the Church we grow in holiness, especially through prayer, good works, and the celebration of the sacraments.

The Church is *catholic*. The word *catholic* means "universal." The Church is universal, or open to all people, since everyone is invited and welcomed to become members of the Church. All people are invited to be followers of Jesus Christ. Today there are Catholics on every continent and in every country of the world.

The Church is *apostolic*. This means that the Church was built on the faith of the Apostles and continues to be guided by their successors, the bishops. The Church is apostolic today because the life and leadership of the Church is based on that of the Apostles' mission which was given to them by Jesus. As baptized Catholics, disciples of Jesus, we, too, share in the work of spreading the Good News of Jesus Christ to all the world.

In your own words describe what each of the Marks of the Church means.

3 Catholics worship and serve together.

A **parish** is a community of believers. It is made up of Catholics who usually live in the same town or neighborhood. A parish is part of a diocese. Members of a parish gather together in Jesus' name to worship God and to share with one another.

In parishes, members gather together to:

- celebrate Mass and the other sacraments
- pray and grow in their faith
- share what they have—money, time, talents—with one another
- care for people in need—those who are sick, poor, or hungry.

Priests work in the parishes of a diocese. **Priests** preach the Gospel and serve the faithful, especially by celebrating the Eucharist and the other sacraments. They are baptized men who have been ordained to this ministry in the Sacrament of Holy Orders. Priests work with the bishop of their diocese. A **pastor** is the priest who leads

the parish in worship, prayer, teaching, and service. His most important work is to lead the parish in the celebration of Mass. A parish might also have other priests who work with the pastor.

Sometimes a parish has a deacon. A **deacon** is a baptized man who in the Sacrament of Holy Orders has been ordained to serve the Church by preaching, baptizing, performing marriages, and doing acts of charity. He carries on his responsibilities under the authority of the bishop and in cooperation with the bishop and his priests.

In many parishes lay people, men and women who are not ordained, serve in various roles. Lay ecclesial ministers are lay people who serve in leadership positions and are recognized and appointed by the Church.

It is important to remember that each person is an important part of the parish.

How will you participate in the parish community this week?

Review

Write *True* or *False* next to the following sentences. On a separate piece of paper, change the false sentences to make them true.

1. _____ The word *catholic* means "founded on the Apostles."

2. _____ The pope continues the leadership of the Apostle Peter.

3. _____ The successors of the Apostles were given the title *deacon*.

4. _____ The Catholic Church is only open to a certain number of people.

Discuss the following.

5. How did the Apostles give their successors the authority Jesus had given to them?

6. Name the four Marks of the Church and briefly describe each one.

7. For what reasons do parish members come together?

Faith Words

bishops (page 34)

diocese (page 34)

pope (page 34)

Marks of the Church (page 35)

parish (page 36)

priests (page 36)

pastor (page 36)

deacon (page 36)

With My Family
Sharing Our Faith

1 The pope and bishops are the successors of the Apostles.

2 The Church is one, holy, catholic, and apostolic.

3 Catholics worship and serve together.

PRAYING TOGETHER

As you pray Psalm 117, think about all the members of the Church who live in every country of the world.

"Praise the LORD, all you nations!
Give glory, all you peoples!
The LORD's love for us is strong;
the LORD is faithful forever.
Hallelujah!" (Psalm 117:1–2)

• •˙ Living Our Faith • •˙

This week think about ways you can participate in your parish. Decide on one or two ways that you will actually participate. Write these ways below.

_____

_____

Remember that one important way to participate in your parish is to pray for parish members, especially the people in need. Complete the following prayer.

Jesus, bless the members of our parish.

_____

_____

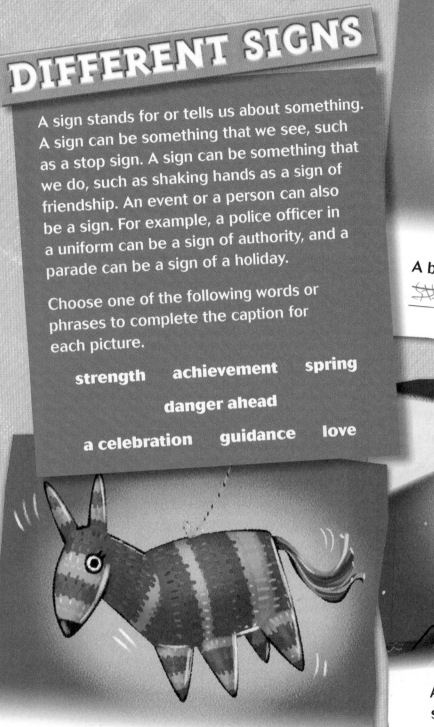

DIFFERENT SIGNS

A sign stands for or tells us about something. A sign can be something that we see, such as a stop sign. A sign can be something that we do, such as shaking hands as a sign of friendship. An event or a person can also be a sign. For example, a police officer in a uniform can be a sign of authority, and a parade can be a sign of a holiday.

Choose one of the following words or phrases to complete the caption for each picture.

strength   achievement   spring

danger ahead

a celebration   guidance   love

A blaring whistle can be a sign of
~~STOP~~ Danger ahead

A light from a lighthouse can be a sign of
Land

A piñata can be a sign of
celebration

A rock can be a sign of

_I D K_

A blue ribbon is a sign of

wining

Giving someone a hug can be a sign of

Love

Budding flowers can be a sign of

Smely

We Will Learn...

1 Jesus is the greatest sign of God's love.

2 The Church celebrates seven special signs, the sacraments.

3 The sacraments unite us as the Body of Christ.

1 Jesus is the greatest sign of God's love.

Jesus Christ is the Son of God. Everything that Jesus said or did pointed to God's love for us. So all of Jesus' words and actions are signs of God's love. In the Gospels we read about these words and actions. We read about:

- ways that Jesus opened his arms and welcomed all

- ways that Jesus spent time with people whom others disliked or neglected

- ways that Jesus fed those who were hungry

- ways that Jesus touched people and healed them both physically and spiritually

- ways that Jesus comforted sinners and forgave their sins

- the way that Jesus gave his life to save us all from sin.

For all of these reasons Jesus is the greatest sign of his Father's love.

Jesus knew that his disciples needed him to be present with them. Yet he would have to leave them and return to his Father in Heaven. So Jesus promised them that he would always be with them through the power of the Holy Spirit.

In what ways did Jesus show people God's love for them?

2 The Church celebrates seven special signs, the sacraments.

Over time, the Catholic Church recognized certain symbolic actions as signs of the risen Christ made present in the community through the power of the Holy Spirit. Eventually the Church named seven of these actions or signs it had received from Jesus Christ as the Seven Sacraments. These Seven Sacraments are Baptism, Confirmation, Eucharist, Penance and Reconciliation, Anointing of the Sick, Holy Orders, and Matrimony.

All Seven Sacraments are signs of God's presence in our lives. But sacraments are different from all other signs. They are effective signs which means that they truly bring about what they represent. For example, in Baptism we not only celebrate being children of God, we actually become children of God. In Penance and Reconciliation we not only celebrate that God forgives, we actually receive God's forgiveness.

This is why we say that a **sacrament** is an effective sign given to us by Jesus Christ through which we share in God's life. This gift of God's life in us is **grace**. Through the Holy Spirit we receive grace in each sacrament. This grace, called *sanctifying grace*, heals us of sin and helps us to grow in holiness. As God's goodness and holiness grows within us, we become more like Jesus. Grace strengthens us to live as Jesus called us to live.

How does the grace we receive in the sacraments help us?

CONFIRMATION

BAPTISM

EUCHARIST

Do You Know?

God freely offers his grace to us in the sacraments. Through the grace we receive in the sacraments, we respond to the presence of God in our lives. We show that we are open to this grace by fully participating in the celebration of each sacrament and by making a commitment to live as disciples of Jesus.

The sacraments unite us as the Body of Christ.

During the celebration of the sacraments, Christ is joined in a special way with the Church. The Church, the whole Body of Christ, celebrates each sacrament. The priest and other members of the Church who participate in the sacraments represent the whole Church. The sacraments unite Catholics all over the world with Jesus and with one another.

There are three groups of sacraments: Sacraments of Christian Initiation, Sacraments of Healing, and Sacraments at the Service of Communion.

- The Sacraments of Christian Initiation are Baptism, Confirmation, and the Eucharist. Through these sacraments we are born into the Church, strengthened, and nourished.

- The Sacraments of Healing are Penance and Reconciliation, and Anointing of the Sick. Through them we experience God's forgiveness, peace, and healing.

- The Sacraments at the Service of Communion are Holy Orders and Matrimony. In Holy Orders a baptized man is consecrated and in Matrimony a man and woman are blessed to serve God and the Church through a particular vocation.

It is through the grace that we receive in the sacraments that we are able to respond to the presence of God in our lives.

Which sacraments have you received?

PENANCE

MATRIMONY

ANOINTING of the SICK

HOLY ORDERS

42

Choose a phrase to complete each sentence.

> Christian Initiation   effective signs
> God's life   the Holy Spirit

1. The sacraments are

   _____

   given to us by Jesus Christ through which we share in God's life.

2. Through the Sacraments of

   _____

   we are born into the Church, strengthened, and nourished.

3. Grace is our share in

   _____ .

4. Jesus' presence continued in the disciples' lives through the power of

   _____ .

Discuss the following.

5. Why is Jesus the greatest sign of God's love?

6. How are the Seven Sacraments different from all other signs?

7. What are the three groups of sacraments?

Faith Words

sacrament (page 41)

grace (page 41)

With My Family

Sharing Our Faith

1 Jesus is the greatest sign of God's love.

2 The Church celebrates seven special signs, the sacraments.

3 The sacraments unite us as the Body of Christ.

PRAYING TOGETHER

Pray the following prayer for the people in your parish who are preparing to receive the sacraments.

God our Father, you gave us your only Son
who is the greatest sign of your love.
Be with the people in our parish
who are preparing to receive the sacraments.
Jesus, help them to remember that you are present with them
as they celebrate these sacraments.
Holy Spirit, help each person be open to the grace
he or she will receive in the sacrament.
We ask this through Christ our Lord. Amen.

Living Our Faith

In this chapter you have learned about the Seven Sacraments. This week talk with your family about the sacraments each of you has received. As you discuss, list the celebrations here.

_____

_____

MORE for You to Know

DEPOSIT OF FAITH The Deposit of Faith is all the truth contained in Scripture and Tradition. Jesus Christ revealed and entrusted this truth to the Apostles. They, in turn, entrusted this truth to their successors, the bishops, and the entire Church.

It is within the Church, the community of faith, that we discover the truth. The Magisterium, the living teaching office of the Church, guides us in understanding the truth. The Magisterium consists of the pope and bishops. They teach us the correct understanding of the message of Scripture and Tradition and ways to live out this message.

In each generation, the whole Church continues to share and build upon the faith of the Apostles. With the guidance of the Holy Spirit, the Church hands on all the truths she has received through God's Revelation. The Church's faith is always developing, and God's Revelation is living and active in the Church.

INFALLIBILITY Infallibility is the gift of the Holy Spirit that keeps the Church free from error—in her beliefs and teachings—in matters concerning Divine Revelation and the Deposit of Faith. The pope also has the gift of infallibilty when he defines a truth pertaining to faith and morals.

THE LORD'S PRAYER During the Sermon on the Mount, Jesus taught his followers the Lord's Prayer, a prayer to God the Father. This prayer is an essential prayer of the Church—integrated into her liturgical prayer and sacraments.

In the first part of the Lord's Prayer, we give glory to God, we pray for the coming of God's Kingdom, and we pray to God for the ability to do his will.

In the second part of the Lord's Prayer, we ask God for everything we need for ourselves and for the world. We ask God to heal us of our sin. We pray that God will protect us from all that could draw us away from his love. We ask God to guide us in choosing good in our lives, and we ask him for the strength to follow his law.

Circle the correct answer.

1. The Church celebrates (**three/seven/four**) Sacraments of Christian Initiation.

2. There are (**nine/seven/four**) Marks of the Church.

3. On Pentecost, Peter spoke to the crowd and (**only a few/only twelve/ about three thousand**) people were baptized.

4. The Church is catholic, open to (**all/some/many**) people.

5. (**Each person, Only the pastor, Only the deacon**) is important to the parish.

Complete the following statements.

6. The _____ and the bishops continue the leadership of the Apostle Peter and the other Apostles.

7. The Catholic Church has four Marks: one, _____, catholic, and apostolic.

8. A _____ is an effective sign given to us by Jesus Christ through which we share in God's life.

9. The _____, the whole Body of Christ, celebrates each sacrament.

10. Through the Sacraments of _____ we are born into the Church, strengthened, and nourished.

Write your responses on a separate sheet of paper.

11. Write one reason why Jesus sent the Holy Spirit to his disciples.

12. Choose one of the four Marks of the Church and explain its meaning.

13. Identify ways Jesus showed his disciples that he is the greatest sign of God's love.

14. What is the Church?

15. Name two ways in which you can participate in your parish.

Circle the letter of the correct answer.

1. The truth that God the Son became man is _____.
   a. the Resurrection
   b. the Ascension
   c. Pentecost
   d. the Incarnation

2. One of the Sacraments of Christian Initiation is _____.
   a. Matrimony
   b. Confirmation
   c. Anointing of the Sick
   d. Holy Orders

3. The people who serve in a parish are _____.
   a. deacons
   b. lay people
   c. priests
   d. all of the above

4. Jesus' return in all his glory to his Father in Heaven is called _____.
   a. the Resurrection
   b. the Ascension
   c. Pentecost
   d. the Incarnation

5. The Church is _____. This means that the Church is universal, open to all people.
   a. one
   b. holy
   c. catholic
   d. apostolic

Complete the following.

6. The greatest sign of God's love is _____
   _____.

7. God's plan for human beings was that _____
   _____.

8. The Apostles are the _____

_____ .

9. Jesus told his followers that the Kingdom of God is like a _____

_____ .

10. Through the grace we receive in each sacrament, _____

_____ .

Circle the correct answer.

11. The Sacrament of Penance and Reconciliation is a Sacrament of (**Healing, Christian Initiation**).

12. Each local area of the Church is called a (**deacon, diocese**).

13. A (**diocese, sacrament**) is an effective sign because it truly brings about what it represents.

14. The day the Holy Spirit came upon Jesus' disciples is called (**Easter Sunday, Pentecost**). It was on this day that the Church began.

15. Jesus Christ is (**only divine, divine and human**).

Write your responses.

16. What did Jesus do for his disciples at the Last Supper?

_____

17. What is the role of the pope and bishops?

_____

18. Name the Marks of the Church. Choose one and describe what it means.

_____

19. What is the Kingdom of God?

_____

20. Write two ways you can participate in your parish community.

_____

Welcome Michael!

My Baptism

My cousins making my banner

Hello. My name is Margaret. Yesterday I asked Dad questions about my Baptism: Who was there? Where was I baptized? What did everyone do after the Baptism? To help answer my questions, Dad found our family's treasure box. In the box we found many things from the day I was baptized: photographs, my baptismal certificate, a banner, and many other baptismal keepsakes.

I wanted to know about my Baptism because my Aunt Melissa and Uncle Kyle just adopted a baby. The baby's name is Michael, and he is going to be baptized. My parents and I, my grandparents, aunts, uncles, and cousins are going to my Aunt Melissa's parish church to celebrate Michael's Baptism. After the Baptism we are invited to my grandparents' house for a party.

Party after my Baptism

I asked Mom what I could do for Michael. Mom handed me the banner that was in our box and said, "Margaret, your twin cousins made this and gave it to you on the day of your Baptism." When I opened the banner, it was brightly decorated and had "Welcome, Margaret" printed in large letters. After seeing my banner, I decided to make a banner for Michael.

In the space above, help Margaret decorate her banner.

Who was at the celebration of your Baptism?

Have you ever been to a baptismal celebration of a family member or friend?

What do you remember about the celebration?

We Will Learn...

1 Baptism is the foundation of the Christian life.

2 We celebrate the Sacrament of Baptism.

3 We celebrate the Sacrament of Confirmation.

Baptism is the foundation of the Christian life.

Baptism is the first sacrament that we celebrate. In fact, we are unable to receive any other sacrament until we have first been baptized. Through Baptism we receive a share in God's own life, the life of grace. The grace of Baptism makes us children of God, members of Christ, and Temples of the Holy Spirit. It gives us the power to live and act as disciples of Jesus Christ.

Baptism leads us to the other two Sacraments of Christian Initiation, Confirmation and Eucharist. **Baptism** is the sacrament in which we:

- *Are freed from sin:* Jesus' victory over sin and death offers us Salvation. Salvation is the forgiveness of sins and the restoring of friendship with God. Baptism is necessary for Salvation. Baptism frees us from Original Sin and all our personal sins are forgiven.

- *Become children of God:* We become sisters and brothers with everyone else who has been baptized. Baptism makes us members of one family. God sees all of us as his children. He loves each one of us.

- *Are welcomed into the Church:* At Baptism we are welcomed into a community of believers led by the Holy Spirit. We become a part of the Body of Christ, the People of God. We are united with all those who have been baptized in Christ.

What are three things that happen when we are baptized?

Do You Know?

At Baptism we are sealed, or marked forever, as belonging to Jesus Christ. This spiritual mark, called a character, can never be erased. Once we have received Baptism, no matter what may happen, we belong to Christ and the Church. Thus, Baptism is a sacrament that is never repeated. Once we have been baptized, we are marked forever with the sign of faith and have the hope of eternal life, living in happiness with God forever.

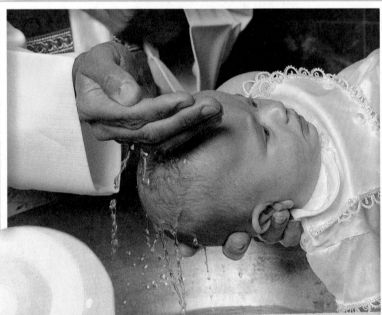

2 We celebrate the Sacrament of Baptism.

Many people are baptized as infants or young children. Others are baptized as older children, adolescents, or adults. No one is ever too young or too old to begin a new life in Christ through Baptism.

In many parishes infants or young children receive the Sacrament of Baptism on Sunday, the day of Jesus Christ's Resurrection. The celebration of the sacrament on Sunday highlights the fact that through Baptism we rise to new life in Christ. The Sunday celebration allows parish members to participate in the celebration. The **celebrant** of Baptism is a bishop, priest, or deacon. He celebrates the sacrament for and with the community. Because Baptism is necessary for Salvation, when there is a serious need, anyone can baptize.

The actual Baptism can take place in two ways. The celebrant can immerse, or plunge, the child in water three times. Or the celebrant can pour water over the child's head three times.

While immersing or pouring, the celebrant says,

"N.[name], I baptize you in the name
   of the Father,
and of the Son,
and of the Holy Spirit."

Chrism is perfumed oil blessed by the bishop. The celebrant anoints the newly-baptized child on the crown of the head with Chrism. This anointing is a sign of the Gift of the Holy Spirit. It shows that the newly-baptized child shares in the mission of Jesus Christ. This anointing also connects Baptism to the Sacrament of Confirmation during which another anointing with Chrism takes place.

When were you baptized?

Who took part in the celebration?

We celebrate the Sacrament of Confirmation.

Confirmation is the sacrament in which we receive the Gift of the Holy Spirit in a special way. Confirmation is a Sacrament of Christian Initiation. Confirmation strengthens our bond with Christ and the Church. All baptized members of the Church are called to receive this sacrament.

A bishop from the diocese comes to the parish to confirm the candidates, often during a special Mass. When necessary, a bishop may designate a priest to confirm the candidates.

The bishop confirms each candidate by laying his right hand on the candidate's head and tracing the Sign of the Cross on the candidate's forehead with Chrism.

As the bishop does this he calls the candidate by name, saying, "Be sealed with the Gift of the Holy Spirit."

The person confirmed responds, "Amen."

At Confirmation, the anointing with Chrism confirms and completes the baptismal anointing. Like the character or mark of Baptism, the seal of Confirmation is with a person always. Because of this, a person receives Confirmation only once.

Those who are baptized as adults or older children often receive Baptism, Confirmation, and the Eucharist at one celebration, usually at the Easter Vigil. Those who are baptized as infants or young children usually receive Confirmation between the ages of seven and sixteen.

The parish community helps young people prepare for Confirmation through prayer, instruction in the faith, and opportunities for service. The people who are to be confirmed are called candidates. Candidates must profess their faith, be without serious sin, desire Confirmation, and be ready to live their faith.

When we are baptized, the Holy Spirit shares seven spiritual gifts with us to help us to live as faithful followers of Jesus Christ. At Confirmation the Holy Spirit strengthens these gifts within us so that throughout our lives we can be witnesses to our faith in our words and actions. The Gifts of the Holy Spirit are: wisdom, understanding, counsel (right judgment), fortitude (courage), knowledge, piety (reverence), and fear of the Lord (wonder and awe).

How does a person prepare for the Sacrament of Confirmation?

Write *True* or *False* next to the following sentences. On a separate piece of paper, change the false sentences to make them true.

1. _____ At Baptism we are freed from Original Sin.

2. _____ We may receive the Sacrament of Confirmation more than once.

3. _____ We celebrate the Sacraments of Baptism and Confirmation in private.

4. _____ At Baptism and Confirmation a person is anointed with Chrism.

Discuss the following.

5. Why is it appropriate for parish communities to celebrate Baptism on Sunday?

6. What do we become at Baptism?

7. What do the seven Gifts of the Holy Spirit help us to do?

Faith Words

Baptism (page 50)

celebrant (page 51)

Chrism (page 51)

Confirmation (page 52)

With My Family

Sharing Our Faith

1 Baptism is the foundation of the Christian life.

2 We celebrate the Sacrament of Baptism.

3 We celebrate the Sacrament of Confirmation.

PRAYING TOGETHER

As you pray, reflect on how wonderful it is to share in God's life, the life of grace.

Lord,
fulfill your promise.
Send your Holy Spirit
to make us witnesses before the world
to the good news proclaimed by Jesus
Christ, our Lord. (Rite of Confirmation)

• Living Our Faith •

At Baptism you receive seven Gifts of the Holy Spirit. Read a brief description of each of these gifts found on page 115 of this book. Then choose two of these gifts and write how each can help you live as a child of God and member of the Church.

_____

_____

_____

_____

_____

Gifts to Treasure

Last Saturday Eric went to his Grandmom Lily's house to help her pack. She was going to move to a neighboring town. When Eric got to the house, Grandmom Lily was in the kitchen. She was going through boxes that she had brought up from the basement. Grandmom Lily said to Eric, "Look at two treasures I just found."

Eric thought his grandmother was going to show him a necklace or some other pieces of jewelry. But Grandmom Lily handed him a book of coupons. She said, "When your father was your age, he gave me these coupons for my birthday."

Eric laughed when he read the coupons aloud. The first one read, "I will clean my room before you ask me." Another one read, "I will not complain once this week."

Then Grandmom Lily held up a seashell. She told Eric, "Your Aunt Lee gave this shell to me that same year. It was her favorite shell from the collection she had. Out of all the birthday gifts I received that year, these two were my favorites."

Eric asked, "Why were these gifts your favorites, Grandmom?"

Grandmom Lily answered, "Because they were gifts of love. Eric, always remember that some of the most meaningful gifts you can give cannot be bought in a store. When we love others, we give them our time and attention. We listen to them. We spend time with them. We try to help them. In fact, you're giving me a gift right now—the gift of your time and love."

Eric's grandmother put the coupons and the shell in a small box. She said, "I'm going to make room for these two treasures in my new home."

What is the most meaningful gift someone has given to you?

What is the most meaningful gift you have given to someone?

We Will Learn...

1 Jesus gave us himself in the Eucharist.

2 The Eucharist is a memorial, a meal, and a sacrifice.

3 The Mass is the celebration of the Eucharist.

1 Jesus gave us himself in the Eucharist.

Jesus wanted to remain present with his disciples. So at the Last Supper on the night before he died, Jesus gave his disciples a special way to remember him and to be with him. "While they were eating, he took bread, said the blessing, broke it, and gave it to them, and said, 'Take it; this is my body.' Then he took a cup, gave thanks, and gave it to them, and they all drank from it. He said to them, 'This is my blood of the covenant, which will be shed for many.'" (Mark 14:22–24)

Jesus' breaking of the bread and sharing of the cup was an offering of himself for our Salvation. At the Last Supper Jesus gave us the gift of himself and instituted the Eucharist. Through the Eucharist Jesus remains with us forever.

The **Eucharist** is the sacrament of the Body and Blood of Christ. The Mass is the celebration of the Eucharist.

Through the power of the Holy Spirit and the words and actions of the priest, Jesus truly becomes present to us in the Sacrament of the Eucharist. He is truly present to us under the appearances of bread and wine. We receive Jesus Christ himself in Holy Communion.

When we receive the Eucharist, we share in God's own life—the life of the Father, the Son, and the Holy Spirit. Our relationship with Christ and one another is strengthened. Christ unites all the faithful in one body, the Body of Christ, the Church.

In the Sacrament of the Eucharist we complete our Christian Initiation into the Church. The Eucharist nourishes us to be faithful members of the Church. Thus, it is the only Sacrament of Christian Initiation that we receive again and again.

Why do you think the Eucharist is at the center of our lives?

2 The Eucharist is a memorial, a meal, and a sacrifice.

The Eucharist is a memorial.

When Jesus gave his disciples the Eucharist, he told them, "do this in memory of me" (Luke 22:19). When we gather and celebrate the Sacrament of the Eucharist, we are remembering Jesus who is present to us in this celebration. We are remembering the new life we have because of Jesus Christ's Death and Resurrection.

The Eucharist is a meal.

At the Last Supper Jesus and his disciples were eating and celebrating a special meal. In the Eucharist we share in a meal. In the Eucharist we, too, are nourished. We are nourished by the Body and Blood of Jesus Christ. As Jesus told us, "For my flesh is true food, and my blood is true drink. Whoever eats my flesh and drinks my blood remains in me and I in him" (John 6:55–56).

The Eucharist is a sacrifice.

A **sacrifice** is a gift offered to God by a priest in the name of all the people. During the celebration of the Eucharist, Jesus acts through the priest. At each celebration, Jesus' sacrifice on the cross, his Resurrection, and his Ascension into Heaven are made present again through the words and actions of the priest.

Through this sacrifice we are saved. This sacrifice is offered for the forgiveness of the sins of the living and the dead. Through it we are reconciled with God and one another. Our less serious sins are forgiven, and we are strengthened to avoid serious sin.

In the Eucharist Jesus offers his Father praise and thanksgiving. This thanks and praise is for all the gifts of Creation. The word *eucharist* means "to give thanks." In every celebration of the Eucharist, the whole Church offers thanks and praise. When we celebrate the Eucharist, we pray to the Father, through the Son, in the unity of the Holy Spirit. We join Jesus in offering ourselves to God the Father. We offer all our joys and concerns. We offer our willingness to live as Jesus' disciples.

What will you remember about Jesus the next time you celebrate the Eucharist?

What joys and concerns will you offer to God?

The Mass is the celebration of the Eucharist.

The Mass is the Church's great act of worship. The celebration of the Eucharist, the Mass, is the center of the Church's life. For this reason the Church requires all members to participate in Mass every Sunday or Saturday evening.

When we participate in the Mass, we show that we appreciate the great gift Jesus has given us—the gift of himself. Some of the ways that we participate are by singing, praying the responses, listening and responding to readings from the Bible, and receiving Holy Communion.

During Mass Jesus is among us. He offers himself so that we can grow in God's friendship and love. Jesus is present to us in the Word of God, in those who have gathered in his name, in the priest celebrant, and most importantly, in his Body and Blood which we receive in Holy Communion.

The Church recommends that each time we participate in the Mass, we receive Holy Communion. The Church requires us to receive Holy Communion at least once a year.

How will you participate in next Sunday's Mass?

Do You Know?

The Church has many feast days, including very special ones called Holy Days of Obligation. The Church requires that we participate in Mass on these days. In addition to Sundays, in the United States the Holy Days of Obligation are:

Solemnity of Mary, Mother of God (January 1)

Ascension (when celebrated on Thursday during the Easter season)

Assumption of Mary (August 15)

All Saints' Day (November 1)

Immaculate Conception (December 8)

Christmas (December 25)

Complete the following sentences.

1. Jesus gave us the gift of himself in the Eucharist at _____ _____ .

2. The word *eucharist* means " _____ ."

3. In the Eucharist Jesus is truly present to us under the appearances of _____ .

4. The Eucharist is a memorial, a meal, and a _____ .

Discuss the following.

5. What happens to us when we receive the Eucharist?

6. How is Jesus present to us at Mass?

7. In what ways do we participate at Mass?

Faith Words

Eucharist (page 56)

sacrifice (page 57)

With My Family

Sharing Our Faith

 1 Jesus gave us himself in the Eucharist.

 2 The Eucharist is a memorial, a meal, and a sacrifice.

 3 The Mass is the celebration of the Eucharist.

PRAYING TOGETHER

After we receive Jesus in Holy Communion, we can say the following prayer of thanks.

Jesus,
thank you for coming to me in Communion.
Thank you for strengthening me to be your disciple and to serve others.
Help me to be grateful for each day and to stay close to you always.
Amen.

Living Our Faith

In this chapter you have learned that the Mass is a celebration of praise and thanksgiving. Discuss what gifts from God you are most grateful for this week. Write these gifts below. Then write ways you can show God your thanks.

Gift	Way to give thanks
Our food	Try not to waste food. Donate food to a pantry.
_____	_____
_____	_____
_____	_____

Family Celebrations

Think about your family's celebrations.

Which recent celebration was your favorite?

_____

When was the celebration?

_____

Who was there?

_____

_____

_____

_____

Check the celebration activities in which you participated. Add your own.

_____ sharing a meal

_____ telling family stories

_____ listening to family stories

_____ singing

_____ dancing

_____ taking photos or a video

_____ _____

How will you remember the celebration?

_____ look at photos or watch the video

_____ make scrapbook pages

_____ write about the celebration in a diary or journal

_____ talk about the celebration with family and friends

We Will Learn...

1 At Mass we praise God, and we listen to his Word.

2 We offer gifts, and the Eucharistic Prayer begins.

3 We receive Holy Communion, and we are sent to bring God's love to others.

1 At Mass we praise God, and we listen to his Word.

The Mass is the celebration of the Eucharist. The community of people who gather for this celebration is called the liturgical **assembly**. Only an ordained priest can preside at Mass. He leads the assembly in the celebration of the Mass. The Mass has four parts: the Introductory Rites, the Liturgy of the Word, the Liturgy of the Eucharist, and the Concluding Rites.

The part of the Mass that unites us as a community is the **Introductory Rites**. It prepares us to hear God's Word and to celebrate the Eucharist. During the Introductory Rites, we make the Sign of the Cross with the priest, who greets us in Jesus' name. Together we recall our sins and ask for God's mercy. Then, on most Sundays of the year, we praise God by saying or singing the Gloria—a prayer giving glory to God. The priest prays the Opening Prayer, known as the *Collect*. It is prayed to God the Father through Christ in the Holy Spirit.

Then we participate in the **Liturgy of the Word**, which is the part of the Mass when we listen and respond to God's Word. We hear about God's great love for his people. We hear about the life and teaching of Jesus Christ. On Sunday, we listen to three readings from the Bible, the Word of God.

• The first reading is usually from the Old Testament. We respond to this reading by singing or praying a psalm.

• The second reading is from the New Testament, most often from one of the letters of Saint Paul.

• The last reading is always taken from one of the four Gospels. These are accounts of the Good News of Jesus Christ in the New Testament according to: Matthew, Mark, Luke, or John. We stand to listen as the priest or deacon proclaims the Gospel.

After the readings and the Gospel, the priest, or deacon gives a *homily*. We listen as he explains the meaning of the readings and teaches us about our Catholic faith. Then, together, we say the Creed, stating our beliefs in God and in all that the Church teaches. Next, we pray together the Prayer of the Faithful for the needs of the Church, the world, and our local community.

How would you explain the Introductory Rites and the Liturgy of the Word to a younger child?

2 We offer gifts, and the Eucharistic Prayer begins.

The Liturgy of the Eucharist is the third part of the Mass. The **Liturgy of the Eucharist** is the part of the Mass when the bread and wine become the Body and Blood of Christ, which we receive in Holy Communion.

The Liturgy of the Eucharist begins as the deacon or priest prepares the altar and the gifts that we offer. Members of the assembly present to the priest gifts of wheat bread and grape wine and our collection for the Church and the poor. These gifts are a sign that we give to God all that we are and all that we do. The priest then gives thanks to God for the gifts. We respond, "Blessed be God for ever."

Then the priest in the name of the entire community prays the Eucharistic Prayer, the Church's greatest prayer of praise and thanksgiving.

During this prayer the priest says and does what Jesus said and did at the Last Supper. As the priest takes the bread, he says,

"TAKE THIS, ALL OF YOU, AND EAT OF IT, FOR THIS IS MY BODY, WHICH WILL BE GIVEN UP FOR YOU."

As the priest takes the cup of wine, he says:

"TAKE THIS, ALL OF YOU, AND DRINK FROM IT, FOR THIS IS THE CHALICE OF MY BLOOD…."

This part of the Eucharistic Prayer is called the *Consecration*. Through these words and actions of the priest, by the power of the Holy Spirit, the bread and wine become the Body and Blood of Christ. This change that the bread and wine undergo is called *transubstantiation*.

At the end of the Eucharistic Prayer, we say or sing "Amen." Together we are saying "Yes, we believe."

Explain what happens during the Eucharistic Prayer.

We receive Holy Communion, and we are sent to bring God's love to others.

The Liturgy of the Eucharist continues as we prepare to receive Jesus Christ in Holy Communion. Together we pray the Lord's Prayer, also called the Our Father. We offer a Sign of Peace to each other. We say aloud or sing the Lamb of God, asking for God's mercy and peace. Then the priest breaks the large Host.

At the proper time we come forward to receive Holy Communion. We sing to show our unity with Christ and one another. We receive the Body and Blood of Christ in Holy Communion.

During the last part of Mass, the **Concluding Rites**, the priest blesses us. Then he or the deacon says these or similar words, "Go and announce the Gospel of the Lord."

We have been nourished by the celebration of the Eucharist. Now we are sent to love and serve the Lord each day by bringing the peace and love of Jesus to everyone we meet. We can share our time and talents. We can care for the poor, sick, and lonely people we see around us. As members of the Church, we are called to share the Gospel of Jesus Christ with those around us. This is what it means to live the message of the Eucharist we have celebrated, and what it means to be followers of Christ.

How will you share your time and talents with others this week?

Do You Know?

The Church urges us to receive Holy Communion each time we participate in the Mass. To receive Holy Communion we must be in the state of grace. Therefore, if we have committed serious sin, we must first receive God's forgiveness in the Sacrament of Penance.

The Church requires us to receive Communion at least once a year. When we receive Communion, our unity with Jesus Christ and the Church, the Body of Christ, is strengthened.

Saint Benedict Catholic Church

Complete the following sentences by writing the correct part of the Mass.

1. Members of the assembly present gifts of bread and wine during the

   _____ .

2. We sing or say the Gloria during the

   _____ .

3. We are sent to serve God and others

   during the _____ .

4. Bread and wine become the Body and Blood of Christ during the

   _____ .

5. The priest or deacon proclaims the

   Gospel during the _____ .

Discuss the following.

6. Explain what happens during the Introductory Rites of Mass.

7. Explain what happens during the Liturgy of the Word.

8. Explain what happens during the Liturgy of the Eucharist.

assembly (page 62)

Introductory Rites (page 62)

Liturgy of the Word (page 62)

Liturgy of the Eucharist (page 63)

Concluding Rites (page 64)

With My Family
Sharing Our Faith

 At Mass we praise God, and we listen to his Word.

 We offer gifts, and the Eucharistic Prayer begins.

3 We receive Holy Communion, and we are sent to bring God's love to others.

PRAYING TOGETHER

At the beginning of the Liturgy of the Eucharist, the priest invites us to lift up our hearts. We respond, "We lift them up to the Lord." Then we praise God by praying or singing:

Holy, Holy, Holy Lord God of hosts.
Heaven and earth are full of your glory.
Hosanna in the highest.
Blessed is he who comes in
    the name of the Lord.
Hosanna in the highest.

Living Our Faith

In the Concluding Rites at Mass, we are sent to live out the message of the Eucharist. Write ways you can do this.

at home

_____

at school

_____

in the neighborhood

_____

MORE for You to Know

THE LITURGY The liturgy is the official public prayer of the Church. The liturgy includes the celebration of the Eucharist and the other sacraments. It also includes the Liturgy of the Hours. We each bring our own selves and our relationship with God to every celebration of the liturgy. We join together as Jesus' true friends and disciples, just as Jesus' first followers did. We proclaim the Good News of Jesus Christ and celebrate his Death and Resurrection. Whenever the liturgy is celebrated, the whole Church is celebrating.

OUR COMMON VOCATION A vocation is a calling to a way of life. As baptized Christians we share a common vocation. Our common vocation is a call from God to grow in holiness and to spread the message of Jesus' life and saving work.

PRIESTHOOD OF THE FAITHFUL When Jesus was baptized by John the Baptist, the Spirit of the Lord came upon him. This baptismal anointing by the Spirit made it known that Jesus Christ is the Messiah, the Anointed One. Jesus' relationship with God his Father was revealed, and God the Holy Spirit came upon Jesus, marking him as Priest, Prophet, and King.

In the Sacrament of Baptism, we too are anointed. We are called to share in Christ's priestly mission. As baptized members of the Church, we share in Christ's priesthood. This priesthood is not the ordained priesthood but is known as the *priesthood of the faithful*.

As sharers in the priesthood of the faithful, we can all participate in the liturgy, especially the Eucharist, in prayer, and in offering our lives to God.

Match the columns.

1. _____ Liturgy of the Eucharist

   a. The priest blesses us, and we go out to bring God's peace and love to others.

2. _____ Liturgy of the Word

   b. We prepare to hear God's Word, and to celebrate the Eucharist as a community.

3. _____ Introductory Rites

   c. The bread and wine become the Body and Blood of Christ which we receive in Holy Communion.

4. _____ Concluding Rites

   d. We listen and respond to God's Word.

Write the term that best fits each statement.

5. During this sacrament the bishop says, "Be sealed with the Gift of the Holy Spirit." _____

6. We are anointed with this oil at both Baptism and Confirmation.

   _____

7. This is the Church's great act of worship. _____

8. Through this sacrament, we become children of God and are freed from sin.

   _____

9. In this sacrament we receive the Body and Blood of Christ. _____

Write your responses on a separate piece of paper.

10. What happens during the Eucharistic Prayer of the Mass?

11. Write two reasons why the Sacrament of Baptism is so important.

12. Name two ways we participate at Mass.

13. What are some ways we can love and serve the Lord?

14. What action connects the Sacraments of Baptism and Confirmation?

15. Why is the celebration of the Eucharist, the Mass, at the center of the Church's life?

Following Rules

What rules might the children in the photographs be following?

What are some rules that you follow at home? in school? in the neighborhood?

How do rules or laws help us?

In the space provided, write about or draw yourself following one of these rules.

We Will Learn...

1 God gave us the Ten Commandments to help us to live in his love.

2 The first three commandments call us to love God.

3 The Fourth through the Tenth Commandments call us to love others and ourselves.

1 God gave us the Ten Commandments to help us to live in his love.

In the Bible we read that God gave the people of Israel the Ten Commandments, or laws, for their safety and freedom. This is the story of the Ten Commandments.

Thousands of years ago the people of Israel lived as slaves in Egypt. But God had chosen the Israelites to be his own people—the ones who would know and worship the one true God. This was hard for them because they were slaves of the Egyptians, who worshiped many false gods. To help the Israelites, God gave them a great leader named Moses.

Through Moses God helped the Israelites escape from Egypt. He led them to safety and freedom in the desert. In return God asked the Israelites to join in a special agreement, or covenant. A **covenant** is a special agreement between God and his people. God said, "If you hearken to my voice and keep my covenant, you shall be my special possession, dearer to me than all other people" (Exodus 19:5).

The people promised to obey God and keep the covenant. Then God gave Moses the laws of the covenant called the **Ten Commandments**. The Ten Commandments would help God's people to remain faithful to the one true God and to be truly safe and free.

How do you think the Ten Commandments help us to be safe and free?

The Ten Commandments	What the Commandments Mean for Us
1. I am the LORD your God: you shall not have strange gods before me.	God must come first in our lives. No person and no thing can be more important to us than God.
2. You shall not take the name of the LORD your God in vain.	We must respect God's name, the name of Jesus, and holy places.
3. Remember to keep holy the LORD'S Day.	We must worship God on Sundays and holy days, and must rest from work.
4. Honor your father and your mother.	We must love, honor, and obey our parents and guardians.
5. You shall not kill.	We must respect and care for the gift of life.
6. You shall not commit adultery.	We must respect our own bodies and the bodies of others in thought, word, and deed.
7. You shall not steal.	We must not take or destroy what belongs to others.
8. You shall not bear false witness against your neighbor.	We must respect the truth.
9. You shall not covet your neighbor's wife.	We must protect the holiness of marriage and the sacredness of human sexuality.
10. You shall not covet your neighbor's goods.	We must respect the rights and property of others.

2 The first three commandments call us to love God.

The First Commandment states that God must come before everyone and everything else in our lives. The Second Commandment reminds us that God's name is holy and must be used with love and respect.

The Third Commandment states that we are to keep holy the Lord's Day. For Catholics, Sunday is the Lord's Day because it was on a Sunday that Jesus Christ rose from the dead. On Sundays we gather with our parish community to celebrate the Mass. Participating in the Mass is the most important way of keeping the Lord's Day holy because the Sacrament of the Eucharist is at the very center of the Christian life. Catholics must participate in Mass on Sunday or Saturday evening and on Holy Days of Obligation. (See list on page 58.)

On Sunday we must also rest from work or other activities so that we can keep the Lord's Day holy.

How does keeping the first three commandments show that you love God?

Do You Know?

When Jesus was growing up in Nazareth, he studied the teachings of the Old Testament. He treasured the covenant God made with his people. He studied the Ten Commandments and obeyed them. When Jesus was older, his followers saw that Jesus lived according to the covenant. One day as Jesus was teaching, he explained, "Do not think that I have come to abolish the law or the prophets. I have come not to abolish but to fulfill" (Matthew 5:17).

3 The Fourth through the Tenth Commandments call us to love others and ourselves.

The Fourth Commandment states that we are to honor our parents. Our parents have given us life. We owe them love, respect, and care. We should also show respect for our guardians, our teachers, older members of the community, and all those in positions of authority.

The Fifth Commandment reminds us that all life is a gift from God, from the moment of conception until natural death. Thus, the Fifth Commandment forbids abortion, suicide, and murder, which includes euthanasia. We must not do anything that would harm others or harm our own bodies and minds.

The Sixth and Ninth Commandments remind us that our human sexuality is something sacred. We must respect our bodies and the bodies of others in thought, word, and deed.

The Seventh Commandment forbids destroying or stealing what belongs to others. We must return items or repay others if we have taken their property. The Tenth Commandment forbids envy, or jealousy of what others own.

The Eighth Commandment requires us to tell the truth. It forbids lying and gossip that hurts others. If we have hurt the good name of others we must try to repair it.

The Ten Commandments show us how to remain faithful to God in this life and to attain eternal life. The commandments help us to live together in peace and love. God has given us these laws for our safety and our freedom.

How does keeping the Fourth through the Tenth Commandments show that you love God and others?

Review

Write *True* or *False* for the following sentences. On a separate piece of paper, change the false sentences to make them true.

1. _____ Through Jesus, God led the Egyptians out of slavery.

2. _____ Catholics keep Sunday as the Lord's Day.

3. _____ When we keep the first three commandments, we are showing love for God.

4. _____ God gave us the Ten Commandments for our safety and our freedom.

Discuss the following.

5. How did the Israelites keep their covenant with God?

6. What are ways we can keep the Lord's Day holy?

7. What are some ways we show love for ourselves and others by keeping the Fourth through the Tenth Commandments?

Faith Words

covenant (page 70)

Ten Commandments (page 70)

With My Family

Sharing Our Faith

 1 God gave us the Ten Commandments to help us to live in his love.

 2 The first three commandments call us to love God.

 3 The Fourth through the Tenth Commandments call us to love others and ourselves.

PRAYING TOGETHER

Pray these words to ask for God's help in obeying God's law.

"Lord, teach me the way of your laws;
  I shall observe them with care.
Give me insight to observe your teaching,
  to keep it with all my heart.
Lead me in the path of your commands,
  for that is my delight."

Psalm 119: 33—35

• Living Our Faith •

Discuss how God's laws are meant to free us to live in peace and harmony with God and one another. Choose two of the commandments, and write ways of keeping each of these commandments at home, in school, at work, and in the neighborhood.

_____

_____

_____

Talk together about following these ways, and how they can promote peace and harmony in your lives.

Camping Out

"Tomorrow's the big day!" Caroline said to her friend Mia when they were having lunch on Friday.

"Yes! My sleeping bag is packed, and I'm ready to go," replied Mia. The two friends were going with the Junior Wilderness Club on their first overnight camping trip. They had been looking forward to it for months.

Later that evening the phone rang at Caroline's apartment. It was Mia. "I can't go camping tomorrow," she whispered. Mia explained that her grandfather had gone into the hospital. Mia said, "Mom is needed at the hospital. She would feel better if I were not so far away. I'm worried about Grandpop, and I don't think I would enjoy the trip. I'll talk to you on Monday. Have a good time."

Caroline told her parents what had happened. Caroline said, "I don't want to go camping now. I won't have any fun without Mia."

Caroline's dad said, "I have an idea. Why don't you invite Mia to spend Saturday night with us? You can camp out here."

Caroline's mom called Mia's mom and said, "On your way to the hospital, you can drop off Mia for a camp out here. I'll call the troop leader and explain." Both Mia and her mom were very happy about this plan.

On Saturday the two girls set up a tent in Caroline's room. They made a giant get-well card for Mia's grandfather. After supper they sang camping songs, and told scary stories.

Before the friends fell asleep, Caroline said, "This is great! I'm sure having fun at our own camp out."

Mia agreed and said, "Caroline, I am so happy that you are my friend. You and your family are helping me and my mom. And I'm sure Grandpop will like the card we made."

. . .

Has something ever happened that you thought would spoil your happiness but instead actually added to it?

What makes you happy?

How can you help others to be happy?

We Will Learn...

1 Jesus teaches his disciples about loving God and others.

2 Jesus teaches us the Beatitudes.

3 We are called to live in faith, hope, and love.

1 Jesus teaches his disciples about loving God and others.

Jesus went from town to town teaching and showing people how much God loves us. He lived by the Ten Commandments and urged his disciples to follow his example. One day someone asked Jesus, "Teacher, which commandment in the law is the greatest?" Jesus said to the man, "You shall love the Lord, your God, with all your heart, with all your soul, and with all your mind" (Matthew 22:36–37). Jesus also told the man, "You shall love your neighbor as yourself" (Matthew 22:39).

We call Jesus' answer the Great Commandment. Following the Great Commandment helps us to show our love for God, ourselves, and others. It helps us find true happiness in the Kingdom of God.

How will you follow the Great Commandment?

2 Jesus teaches us the Beatitudes.

One day many people were gathered to listen to Jesus teach. He taught them the Beatitudes. The **Beatitudes** are Jesus' teachings that describe the way to live as his disciples. When we live as Jesus' disciples, we can find true happiness. In the Beatitudes the word *blessed* means "happy." This is a good clue to what the Beatitudes are all about.

Jesus taught us the Beatitudes as guidelines for being truly happy, and reaching our final goal: life in God's Kingdom forever as his sons and daughters. Look at the chart on this page. It names each Beatitude and states how observing each one helps us to spread the Kingdom of God.

How can we thank Jesus for teaching us ways to find true happiness?

The Beatitudes	What the Beatitudes Mean for Us
"Blessed are the poor in spirit, for theirs is the kingdom of heaven."	We are "poor in spirit" when we depend on God for everything. No person or thing is more important to us than God. We remember that God created us, and our goal in life is to be happy with him forever in Heaven.
"Blessed are they who mourn, for they will be comforted."	We "mourn" when we are sad because of the sin, evil, and suffering in the world. We trust that God will comfort us.
"Blessed are the meek, for they will inherit the land."	We are "meek" when we show respect, gentleness, and patience to all people, even those who do not respect us.
"Blessed are they who hunger and thirst for righteousness, for they will be satisfied."	We "hunger and thirst for righteousness" when we are fair and just toward others.
"Blessed are the merciful, for they will be shown mercy."	We are "merciful" when we are willing to forgive others, and do not take revenge on those who hurt us.
"Blessed are the clean of heart, for they will see God."	We are "clean of heart" when we are faithful to God's teachings, and try to see God in all people and in all situations.
"Blessed are the peacemakers, for they will be called children of God."	We are "peacemakers" when we treat others with love and respect, and when we help others to stop fighting and make peace.
"Blessed are they who are persecuted for the sake of righteousness, for theirs is the kingdom of heaven." Matthew 5:3–10	We are "persecuted for the sake of righteousness" when we are ignored or insulted for following Jesus' example.

We are called to live in faith, hope, and love.

A **virtue** is a good habit that helps us to act according to God's love for us. Virtues help guide our conduct with the help of God's grace. The virtues of faith, hope, and charity are *theological virtues*. They are gifts given to us directly by God.

• **Faith** is the virtue that enables us to believe in God and all that the Church teaches us. We live as people of *faith* by believing in all that God has told us about himself and all that he has done. Faith is necessary in order to be saved. We profess our faith in the words of the Apostles' Creed and by living according to the teachings of Jesus Christ and the Church. The Holy Spirit helps us to have faith in God and to strive for our greatest goal, life forever with God in Heaven.

• **Hope** is the virtue that enables us to trust in God's promise to share his life with us forever. We live as people of *hope* by trusting in Jesus and his promises of the Kingdom of God and of eternal life.

• **Charity**, or love, is the greatest of all virtues. It enables us to love God and to love our neighbor. We live as people of *charity*, or love, by loving God above all things and our neighbors as ourselves.

When we live with faith, hope, and charity, we gradually come to understand and live the happiness that Jesus was teaching in the Beatitudes.

Name one way you can be a person of faith, a person of hope, and a person of charity.

Do You Know?

By our Baptism we are all called to share the Good News of Jesus Christ by what we say and do. This is known as *evangelization.* Evangelization takes place in our everyday lives. Through our words and actions we evangelize those who have not heard the message of Jesus Christ. We can also evangelize those who have heard the message but need encouragement to live out the gift of faith that is theirs.

Fill in the blanks.

1. In the Beatitudes the word

   _____ means "happy."

2. The Beatitudes are teachings of Jesus that describe the way to live as his

   _____ .

3. A _____ is a good habit that helps us to act according to God's love for us.

4. Following the Great Commandment helps us to show our love for

   _____ , _____ ,

   and _____ .

Discuss the following.

5. Choose one of the Beatitudes and explain what it means.

6. How do the virtues of faith, hope, and charity help us to live as disciples of Jesus?

Faith Words

Beatitudes (page 77)

virtue (page 78)

faith (page 78)

hope (page 78)

charity (page 78)

With My Family

Sharing Our Faith

 Jesus teaches his disciples about loving God and others.

 Jesus teaches us the Beatitudes.

 We are called to live in faith, hope, and love.

PRAYING TOGETHER

The following is a traditional prayer of the Church. Read and reflect on the meaning of the words. Pray these words every day this week.

An Act of Love

O Lord God, I love you above all things and I love my neighbor for your sake because you are the highest, infinite and perfect good, worthy of all my love. In this love I intend to live and die. Amen.

Living Our Faith

As a family, identify people you know or have read about who live or lived according to the Beatitudes. Then ask each family member to decide what he or she can do to be more of a "Beatitude person" today. Write some ways here.

_____

_____

_____

_____

BEST FRIENDS

"What's wrong, Carlos? Are you sick?"

When Carlos came home from school, his older sister Gabrielle could tell that something was wrong. Instead of going to the kitchen for a snack, Carlos just sat in the living room.

Carlos answered that he was not sick, but upset at what happened in school.

"Our class was helping Mrs. Fisher move some books in the library. Adam picked up too many books at one time. They slipped out of his hands and fell onto the floor. We all laughed at Adam. Nobody helped him."

"Adam is your best friend. Do you think you hurt his feelings?"

"I guess. Teddy and I called Adam over to our lunch table, but he didn't sit with us. I really think I let Adam down. What should I do?"

Gabrielle told Carlos to call Adam. And that is what he did.

Write what you think the two friends said to each other.

• • •

Have you ever been in the same kind of situation as Carlos and Adam? What did you do?

We Will Learn...

1 Jesus taught us about God's love and forgiveness.

2 We celebrate the Sacrament of Penance and Reconciliation.

3 In the Sacrament of Penance we receive Christ's peace.

Yet, after Baptism, we sometimes make choices that do not show love for God, ourselves, and others. Just as he did two thousand years ago with those who followed him, Jesus today forgives those who are truly sorry. He does this through the Church in the Sacrament of Penance and Reconciliation. We can call this sacrament the Sacrament of Penance. It has also been called the sacrament of conversion, of confession, of forgiveness, and of Reconciliation.

What does it mean to be reconciled with God?

1 Jesus taught us about God's love and forgiveness.

By the way he lived and the things he did, Jesus helped people to turn to God his Father and to follow God's law. Jesus wanted people to turn away from sin and grow closer to God.

During his ministry, Jesus helped his followers turn to God his Father with love and trust. He called them to conversion. **Conversion** is turning back to God with all one's heart. Jesus made their conversion possible by actually forgiving people's sins. They were then reconciled, or brought together again, with God.

As Jesus' followers today, we first receive God's forgiveness in the Sacrament of Baptism. We are freed from Original Sin, and forgiven any personal sins we may have committed. We begin our new life in Jesus Christ.

Do You Know?

We prepare to celebrate the Sacrament of Penance by making an examination of conscience. We think about our choices and determine whether or not we have followed God's law and the teachings and example of Jesus. Doing this helps us to judge our decisions and actions and to know what we need to confess. Serious sins need to be confessed because they completely break our friendship with God. These sins must be forgiven so that we can again share in God's grace. We also confess our less serious sins. The forgiveness of these sins strengthens our weakened friendship with God, and helps us continue loving God and others. If we have committed serious sin, we must receive God's forgiveness in the Sacrament of Penance before receiving Holy Communion.

2 We celebrate the Sacrament of Penance and Reconciliation.

Our **conscience** is our ability to know the difference between good and evil, right and wrong. When we think and do things that lead us away from God or fail to do the good that we can do, we sin. **Sin** is a thought, word, deed, or omission against God's law.

Every sin weakens our friendship with God and can lead to sinful habits. Less serious sin, *venial sin*, does not turn us completely away from God. Very serious sin, *mortal sin*, does completely turn us away from God because it is a choice that we freely make to do something that we know is seriously wrong. If we do not confess mortal sins before we die, we risk eternal separation from God which is called *Hell*.

God never stops loving us, even when we sin. He will always forgive us if we are sorry. We can receive God's forgiveness in the Sacrament of Penance. The sacrament has four main parts:

- **Contrition**—We express our heartfelt sorrow for our sins. We pray an Act of Contrition as a sign of sorrow and intention to sin no more.
- **Confession**—We confess, or tell, our sins to the priest.
- **Penance**—The priest gives us a penance, an action that shows we are sorry for our sins. It is sometimes a prayer or an act of service. Accepting this penance is a sign that we are turning back to God and are willing to change our lives.

- **Absolution**—Our sins are absolved, or forgiven. In the name of Christ and the Church and through the power of the Holy Spirit, a priest grants the forgiveness of sins. As a sign that our sins are being forgiven, the priest extends his hand and prays the words of absolution. We respond, "Amen."

Whether we celebrate the Sacrament of Penance individually or in a communal penance service, we always confess our sins individually to the priest and receive absolution from him. And each time we celebrate the Sacrament of Penance, whether individually or in a group, we are joined to the whole Church.

In the Sacrament of Penance, the priest, who has received the Sacrament of Holy Orders, acts in the name of Jesus Christ and the Church and through the power of the Holy Spirit. So it is important to know that only a priest can hear our confession and forgive our sins. The priest can never, for any reason whatsoever, tell anyone what we have confessed. He has promised to keep the seal of confession.

When the priest is giving us absolution, what does he do as a sign that we are being forgiven?

3 In the Sacrament of Penance we receive Christ's peace.

At the end of the celebration of the Sacrament of Penance, the priest tells us, "Go in peace." We are able to go in peace because our sins have been forgiven. We, in turn, are called to share Christ's peace with others.

One of the ways we share Christ's peace is by forgiving others. Sometimes this is difficult to do. Yet Jesus taught us that we must forgive others. One day when the Apostle Peter asked, "Lord, if my brother sins against me, how often must I forgive him? As many as seven times?" Jesus told him, "I say to you, not seven times but seventy-seven times" (Matthew 18:21, 22). Jesus was telling Peter that he should always be forgiving. And each of us must remember this teaching of Jesus, too!

When we forgive others, we are living out the Beatitude:
"Blessed are the peacemakers,
    for they will be called children of God"
(Matthew 5:9).
By asking for forgiveness and forgiving others, we are following Jesus' teaching. We are showing our love for God and others. And we are spreading Christ's message of peace in our community and throughout the world.

How can you share Christ's peace with others this week?

84

Circle the correct answer.

1. A (penance/contrition/confession) is an action that shows we are sorry for our sins.

2. Our (confession/contrition/conscience) is our ability to know the difference between good and evil, right and wrong.

3. (Some/No/Every) sin weakens our friendship with God.

4. Telling our sins to the priest is (confession/conversion/conscience).

Discuss the following.

5. What do we mean by *conversion*?

6. Why is it important for us to forgive others?

7. What is the role of the priest in the celebration of the Sacrament of Penance?

Faith Words

conversion (page 82)

conscience (page 83)

sin (page 83)

contrition (page 83)

confession (page 83)

penance (page 83)

absolution (page 83)

With My Family

Sharing Our Faith

 Jesus taught us about God's love and forgiveness.

 We celebrate the Sacrament of Penance and Reconciliation.

3 In the Sacrament of Penance we receive Christ's peace.

PRAYING TOGETHER

Here is an Act of Contrition that you can pray while celebrating the Sacrament of Penance or pray at any time.

My God,
I am sorry for my sins with all my heart.
In choosing to do wrong
and failing to do good,
I have sinned against you
whom I should love above all things.
I firmly intend, with your help,
to do penance,
to sin no more,
and to avoid whatever leads me
    to sin.
Our Savior Jesus Christ
suffered and died for us.
In his name, my God, have mercy.

Living Our Faith

The Church teaches that we must form, or educate, our conscience by studying Scripture and the teachings of the Church. As a family, identify one way that you will form your conscience this week.

What to Do?

Complete the following stories.

Last night Cara's little brother was sick. Throughout the night, her parents had taken turns caring for him. This morning Cara noticed that both her mother and father were very tired. Cara decided that

_____

_____

Last week our pastor made a special announcement. He said, "Next week the parish community will have a collection for the families who lost their homes in the downtown fire. Anyone who wishes to help these families may donate clothing, food, or money."

On the way home Matthew Cheng talked with his parents about what the Cheng family would contribute. Matthew and his parents decided that

_____

_____

Family Fund

At Tuesday's meeting of the Protect the Environment Club, Mrs. De Grassi asked the members to participate in a beach sweep. She explained that the club had been asked to clean up Sunset Beach. The sweep would take a few hours. Marissa's best friend, Joanne, said she did not want to participate. Marissa decided that

_____

_____

We Will Learn...

1 Jesus is our greatest example of service to others.

2 We are called to care for the physical needs of others.

3 We are called to care for the spiritual needs of others.

Feed the hungry.

Visit the imprisoned.

Shelter the homeless.

Clothe the naked.

1 Jesus is our greatest example of service to others.

Jesus told his disciples that they should love others as he loved them. And he gave them an example of this love by the way he lived. He cared for those who were in need. He helped those who were sick, visited those who needed his care, and provided food for the hungry.

Jesus told his disciples that at the end of time all of us would be judged by the way we have treated others.

At the Last Judgment at the end of time, Jesus Christ will come again in glory. He will say to those who have led lives of service to others, "For I was hungry and you gave me food, I was thirsty and you gave me drink, a stranger and you welcomed me, naked and you clothed me, ill and you cared for me, in prison and you visited me" (Matthew 25:35–36).

For Jesus tells us, "Amen, I say to you, whatever you did for one of these least brothers of mine, you did for me" (Matthew 25:40).

What can you do this week to show that you are living a life of service to others?

Do You Know?

As disciples of Jesus Christ, we are called to work for justice and peace for all people. We can do this by being a friend to others, especially those who feel lonely or left out. We can treat everyone fairly and help those who are treated unfairly. We can welcome neighbors who are new to our country. We can learn about and care for people who need our help in our own country and throughout the world. We can write to our local and national leaders to ask them to protect the rights and safety of children and all people, especially those in need.

Visit the sick.

Give drink to the thirsty.

Bury the dead.

2 We are called to care for the physical needs of others.

Responding to the needs of others is an important part of our Catholic faith. When we respond to others' needs, we are following Jesus' example of showing mercy. The loving acts that we do to care for the needs of others are called the **Works of Mercy**.

The **Corporal Works of Mercy** are acts of love that help us care for the physical and material needs of others.

Corporal Works of Mercy

- Feed the hungry.
- Give drink to the thirsty.
- Clothe the naked.
- Visit the imprisoned.
- Shelter the homeless.
- Visit the sick.
- Bury the dead.

The Church encourages all members to care for those who are not able to care for themselves. You can check to find out ways your parish community practices the Corporal Works of Mercy.

Bread

Sugar

GIVE

In what ways can you practice the Corporal Works of Mercy?

3 We are called to care for the spiritual needs of others.

Another way that we can care for the needs of others is through the **Spiritual Works of Mercy**. These are acts of love that help us care for the needs of people's hearts, minds, and souls.

Spiritual Works of Mercy

- Admonish the sinner.
  (Give correction to those who need it.)
- Instruct the ignorant.
  (Share our knowledge with others.)
- Counsel the doubtful.
  (Give advice to those who need it.)
- Comfort the sorrowful.
  (Comfort those who suffer.)
- Bear wrongs patiently.
  (Be patient with others.)
- Forgive all injuries.
  (Forgive those who hurt us.)
- Pray for the living and the dead.

Both the Corporal and Spiritual Works of Mercy are important practices of our Catholic faith. We can ask the Holy Spirit to guide us in carrying out these acts of love in our daily lives. When we carry out these Works of Mercy, we are giving witness to Jesus Christ.

Which of the Spiritual Works of Mercy can people your age do? How?

Complete the following.

1–2. Write two Corporal Works of Mercy.

_____

_____

_____

_____

3–4. Write two Spiritual Works of Mercy.

_____

_____

_____

_____

Discuss the following.

5. In what ways did Jesus care for others?

6. Why is it important for us to follow Jesus' example?

7. What will happen at the Last Judgment?

Works of Mercy (page 89)

Corporal Works of Mercy (page 89)

Spiritual Works of Mercy (page 90)

With My Family

Sharing Our Faith

 Jesus is our greatest example of service to others.

 We are called to care for the physical needs of others.

 We are called to care for the spiritual needs of others.

PRAYING TOGETHER

The following prayer is one the Church prays for those who have died.

Eternal rest grant unto them, O Lord,
And let perpetual light shine upon them.
May they rest in peace.
Amen.
May their souls and the souls of all the faithful departed,
through the mercy of God, rest in peace.
Amen.

• ∴ Living Our Faith • •

Think of possible slogans to encourage people to do the Works of Mercy. List them below. Then choose one and on poster board design an ad for a magazine or Web site using your slogan. Share the ad with family and friends.

A Patron Saint

Last Sunday when Juan's family was on the way to Aunt Iris's house, Juan noticed that they were not taking the roads they usually did. He asked, "Where are we going?"

His father explained, "We're going to look at the new church my company has been building."

When the car stopped at the construction site, Juan and his parents got out of the car. Juan's dad said, "The pastor of this new parish is going to be Father Donnelly."

When Father came to the site, he told our team that the bishop announced that the name of the new parish will be Saint John the Baptist."

Juan's mother said, "Saint John the Baptist is your patron saint, Juan. You were born on Saint John's feast day, so your dad and I decided to give you the name Juan, the Spanish name for John."

Juan was surprised. He said, "I know that Saint John was Jesus' cousin, but now I really want to learn more about him."

Then Juan's father said, "When I told Father Donnelly that Saint John was my son's patron saint, he told me that his first name is Sean. Sean is the Irish name for John. And Saint John the Baptist is his patron saint, too."

Later that week, Father Donnelly visited Juan's father's office to see the model of the new parish. Juan and his mother went there to meet him. "Hi Juan," said Father, "let me tell you about our patron saint, John the Baptist!"

• • •

**Who is your patron saint?
your favorite saint?**

What do you know about him or her?

St. John
the
Baptist
Catholic Church

We Will Learn...

1 The Church honors the saints.

2 Mary is Jesus' first disciple and the greatest saint.

3 The Church honors Mary, the Mother of God and the Mother of the Church.

93

1 The Church honors the saints.

Saints are followers of Christ who lived lives of holiness on earth and now share in eternal life with God in Heaven. From the example of the saints' lives, we can learn ways to love God, ourselves, and others. We can learn how to be disciples of Jesus, as they were. Each November 1 the Church honors all the saints in Heaven on the Feast of All Saints. On this day we recall the saints' lives of service and prayer. We remember that their love and prayers for the Church are constant. On this day and throughout the year, we ask the saints to pray to God for us.

As members of the Church, the Body of Christ, we are united to all who have been baptized.

The Communion of Saints is the union of the baptized members of the Church.

- Members on earth respond to God's grace by living a good life and becoming role models for one another.

- Members in Heaven led lives of holiness on earth and now share in the joy of eternal life with God.

- Members in Purgatory are preparing for Heaven, by growing in the holiness necessary to enjoy the happiness of Heaven. The faithful on earth can help them by prayer, especially the Mass, and by offering good works for them.

What saints would you like to learn more about?

Do You Know?

A canonized saint is a person who has been officially named a saint by the Church. The life of this person has been examined by Church leaders. They have decided that this person's life has been an example of faith and holiness. When a person is canonized a saint, his or her name is entered into the worldwide list of saints recognized by the Catholic Church. The following are some of the many canonized saints of the Church:

- Saints Maria and Isidore were married. They worked on a farm in Spain. They cared for God's gifts of Creation and shared the earth's resources with the poor.

- Saint Frances of Rome worked among the poor people of Rome, Italy. She nursed those who suffered from a terrible disease that killed thousands of people.

2 Mary is Jesus' first disciple and the greatest saint.

Mary, the Mother of Jesus, is his first and most faithful disciple. She shares in God's holiness in a very special way because God chose her to be the Mother of his Son. Mary believed in Jesus from the moment that the angel Gabriel told her that God wanted her to be Jesus' Mother. The event at which the announcement was made that Mary would be the Mother of the Son of God is called the **Annunciation**.

Because Mary was to be the Mother of the Son of God, God blessed her in a special way. This special blessing was only given to Mary. God created her free from Original Sin and from all sin since the very first moment of her life, her conception.

This truth about Mary's sinlessness is called the **Immaculate Conception**.

Mary loved Jesus all through his life. She cared for him as he grew. She supported him throughout his ministry. She remained by his side as he died on the cross. She stayed with the Apostles after Jesus' Ascension as they waited for the coming of the Holy Spirit.

Throughout her life Mary trusted in God's will. She had a pure heart and lived a life of holiness. When Mary's work on earth was done, God brought her body and soul to live forever with the risen Christ. This event is known as Mary's **Assumption**.

Why do we consider Mary to be Jesus' first disciple?

Annunciation, Maurice Denis, 1870–1943

Our Lady of Angels, Los Angeles, CA

3 **The Church honors Mary, the Mother of God and the Mother of the Church.**

Mary is special example for all of us. The Church has many titles for Mary. These titles help us to understand Mary's role in our lives and in the life of the Church.

- Blessed Virgin Mary—Mary was not married when the angel told her that she was to be Jesus' Mother. The angel told her that Jesus was to be conceived by the power of the Holy Spirit. And Mary remained a virgin throughout her married life with Joseph. Thus, Mary is known as the Blessed Virgin, the Blessed Virgin Mary, and the Blessed Mother.

- Mother of God—Jesus Christ, the Son of God and Mary's son, is truly human and truly divine. He is the second Person of the Blessed Trinity who became man. Thus, Mary is known as the Mother of God.

- Mother of the Church—As Jesus was dying on the cross, he saw Mary and the Apostle John at his feet. Jesus said to Mary, "Woman, behold, your son." He said to John, "Behold, your mother" (John 19:26, 27). In this way Jesus showed that Mary is the mother of all those who believe and follow him. Thus, Mary is known as the Mother of the Church.

Here are some of the feast days on which the Church honors Mary.

Mary, Mother of God—*January 1*

The Annunciation of Our Lord —*March 25*

The Visitation of the Blessed Virgin Mary—*May 31*

The Assumption of the Blessed Virgin Mary—*August 15*

The Birth of Mary—*September 8*

Immaculate Conception of the Blessed Virgin Mary—*December 8*

Our Lady of Guadalupe—*December 12*

The Church shows love for Mary through devotions and prayer. You will find some of these devotions and prayers in the prayer section of your book (pages 118–123).

Why is Mary so important to the Church?

Write *True* or *False* for the following sentences. On a separate piece of paper, change the false sentences to make them true.

1. _____ The truth that Mary was free from Original Sin from the moment she was conceived is the Immaculate Conception.

2. _____ When Mary's work on earth was done, God brought her body and soul to live with the risen Christ. This is the Annunciation.

3. _____ Joseph announced to Mary that she was to be the Mother of God's Son.

4. _____ Saints are followers of Christ who now share in eternal life with God in Heaven.

Discuss the following.

5. What do you most admire about Mary?

6. Why do we honor the saints?

7. What can you do to learn more about Mary and about the other saints?

Faith Words

saints (page 94)

Communion of Saints (page 94)

Annunciation (page 95)

Immaculate Conception (page 95)

Assumption (page 95)

With My Family
Sharing Our Faith

 1 The Church honors the saints.

 2 Mary is Jesus' first disciple and the greatest saint.

 3 The Church honors Mary, the Mother of God and the Mother of the Church.

PRAYING TOGETHER

The Hail Mary is one of the Church's best known prayers in honor of Mary.

Hail Mary, full of grace,
the Lord is with you!
Blessed are you among women,
and blessed is the fruit
 of your womb, Jesus.
Holy Mary, Mother of God,
pray for us sinners,
now and at the hour of our death. Amen.

Living Our Faith

In this chapter you have learned that Mary and the saints are models of holiness and discipleship. List below your family's favorite saints and/or patron saints. Discuss how these saints show us ways to love God, ourselves, and others and ways we can follow their example.

MORE for You to Know

FORMATION OF CONSCIENCE Failure to form our consciences can result in wrong choices that may be sinful. Certain acts are always wrong and we may never choose to do wrong even if we think good will come from it. We must continue forming our consciences throughout our lives. We can do this by learning all that we can about our faith, and the teachings of the Church; by praying, asking the Holy Spirit to strengthen and guide us; by reading and reflecting on Scripture; by seeking advice from wise, responsible, and faith-filled people; and by examining our consciences often. We must always follow our well-formed consciences.

VIRTUES The theological virtues of faith, hope, and charity are the foundation of the human virtues—habits that come about by our own efforts, with the help of God's grace. Two of the human virtues are chastity and modesty. When we practice the virtue of chastity, we use our

human sexuality in a responsible and faithful way. Jesus Christ is the model of chastity for all of us. Every baptized person is called to lead a chaste life. The virtue of modesty helps us to think, speak, act, and dress in ways that show respect for ourselves and others.

All the human virtues are grouped around the four cardinal virtues. **Prudence** helps us to make good judgments and direct our actions toward what is good. **Justice** helps us to respect the rights of others and give them what is rightfully theirs. **Fortitude** helps us to act bravely in the face of troubles or fears. **Temperance** helps us to keep our desires under control and to balance our use of material goods.

SOCIAL SIN Personal sin can lead to unjust situations and conditions in society that are contrary to God's goodness. This is social sin. Some results of social sin in society are: prejudice, poverty, homelessness, crime, violence, and the destruction of our environment. The Church speaks strongly against social sin.

God wants all of his children to respond to his grace. He calls those who have turned away from him to return to his love and receive his forgiveness, especially in the Sacrament of Penance. When we are sorry for our sins because we believe in God and love him, our sorrow is known as *perfect contrition*. When we are sorry for our sins for other reasons, it is *imperfect contrition*.

ETERNAL LIFE At the moment of death, we are judged by Christ as to how well we loved and served God and others. This is called our *particular judgment*. Those who have lived lives of holiness on earth will immediately share in the joy of Heaven and eternal life. Others whose hearts need to be made perfectly pure will prepare for Heaven in Purgatory. There they will grow in the holiness necessary to enjoy the happiness of Heaven.

Unfortunately, some people have chosen to completely break their friendship with God. They have continually turned away from God's mercy, and have refused his forgiveness. They remain separated from God and do not share in eternal life. This eternal separation from God is called *Hell*. There are those who through no fault of their own do not know Christ or the Church. The Church teaches that such people, who through grace try to seek God and do his will, also have the hope of eternal life.

Write the letter that best defines each term.

1. _d_ covenant

2. _c_ contrition

3. _e_ conscience

4. _b_ charity

5. _a_ Communion of Saints

a. the union of all baptized members of the Church

b. the theological virtue that allows us to love God and others

c. heartfelt sorrow for our sins

d. a special agreement between God and his people

e. our ability to know the difference between right and wrong

Circle the correct answer.

6. The theological virtue that enables us to trust in God's promise to share his life with us forever is (**faith**/**hope**/**charity**).

7. God bringing Mary body and soul to live forever with the risen Christ is known as Mary's (**Annunciation**/**Immaculate Conception**/**Assumption**).

8. The (**First**/**Fourth**/**Fifth**) Commandment is "Honor your father and your mother."

9. Jesus wants us to (**always**/**sometimes**/**never**) forgive others.

10. When we do an action or say a prayer that shows we are sorry for sins, we are doing (**a confession**/**a penance**/**an absolution**).

Write your responses on a separate piece of paper.

11. Write one title of Mary that you have learned about in this unit. Explain its meaning.

12. Explain ways in which we keep the Third Commandment.

13. Name two of the Corporal Works of Mercy. Identify ways you can practice these works during the coming weeks.

14. Write the definition of the Beatitudes.

15. Why is it important for the members of the Church to celebrate the Sacrament of Penance and Reconciliation?

Circle the letter of the correct answer.

1. The sacrament that is the foundation of the Christian life is _____ .
   a. Matrimony
   b. Holy Orders
   c. Penance
   d. Baptism

2. After we hear the readings at Mass, the priest or deacon then _____ .
   a. tells us to leave
   b. asks us questions
   c. prays the Our Father
   d. explains their meaning for our lives

3. The first three commandments tell us _____ .
   a. how good we are
   b. how to make friends
   c. how to love God
   d. when to sing during Mass

4. The Fourth through the Tenth Commandments tell us _____ .
   a. to read the Bible daily
   b. how to love others
   c. how to pray the rosary
   d. how to live a long life

5. The Spiritual Works of Mercy are _____ .
   a. what the priest says at the end of Mass
   b. things our parents make us do at home
   c. actions such as visiting the sick
   d. ways we can care for the needs of people's hearts, minds, and souls

Complete the following.

6. The Beatitudes are Jesus' teachings that describe _____

   _____ .

7. As members of the Church, we respond to the needs of others because _____

   _____ .

8. From the example of Mary and the saints we can learn _____

_____ .

9. We forgive others because _____

_____ .

10. In Holy Communion we receive _____

_____ .

Write the letter to complete each sentence.

11. _____ The Eucharist

a. is strengthened within us at Confirmation.

12. _____ The Gift of the Holy Spirit

b. is turning back to God.

13. _____ The Assumption

c. is the union of all baptized members of the Church.

14. _____ Conversion

d. is the event when God brought Mary body and soul to live forever with the risen Christ.

15. _____ The Communion of Saints

e. is a memorial, a meal, and a sacrifice.

Write your responses on a separate piece of paper.

16. Name two ways we can follow the Third Commandment.

17. What is the Great Commandment?

18. Why did God give us the Ten Commandments?

19. Name the four main parts of the Sacrament of Penance and Reconciliation.

20. Jesus said, "Come, follow me." As a member of the Church, how can you do this?

The Liturgical Year

The liturgy is the official public prayer of the Church. In the liturgy we gather as a community joined to Christ to celebrate what we believe. The Church year is based on the life of Christ and the celebration of his life in the liturgy. So, the Church's year is called the *liturgical year.*

In one liturgical year we recall and celebrate the whole life of Jesus Christ. We celebrate his birth, younger years, his years of teaching and ministry, and most especially his suffering, Death, Resurrection, and Ascension into Heaven.

The readings we hear, the colors we see, and the songs we sing help us to know what season we are celebrating. The liturgical year begins in late November or early December with the season of Advent.

Advent

The season of Advent is a time of joyful preparation. We await the celebration of the Christmas season during which we remember the first coming of the Son of God. We celebrate that God comes into our lives every day. We look forward to Christ's second coming at the end of time. The color for Advent is purple, a sign of expectation.

Christmas

The season of Christmas begins on Christmas Day with the celebration of the birth of the Son of God. During this season we celebrate that God is with us. The color for Christmas is white, a sign of joy.

Lent

Lent is the season in which we strive to grow closer to Jesus through prayer, fasting, and penance. During Lent we pray for and support all who are preparing to receive the Sacraments of Christian Initiation. During Lent we prepare for the Church's greatest celebration. The color for Lent is purple, for penance.

Triduum

The Easter Triduum is the Church's greatest and most important celebration. The word *triduum* means "three days." During these three days, from Holy Thursday evening until Easter Sunday night, we remember Jesus' gift of the Eucharist, his Death, and his Resurrection. The color for Good Friday is red, for Jesus' suffering. The color for the other days of Triduum is white.

Easter

The season of Easter begins on Easter Sunday evening and continues until Pentecost Sunday. During this season we rejoice in the Resurrection of Jesus Christ and the new life he shares with us. We also celebrate Christ's Ascension into Heaven. The color for the Easter season is white, while the color for Pentecost is red and signifies the descent of the Holy Spirit upon the Apostles.

Ordinary Time

The season of Ordinary Time is celebrated in two parts: the first part is between Christmas and Lent, and the second part is between Easter and Advent. During this time we celebrate the whole life of Christ and learn the meaning of living as his disciples. The color for Ordinary Time is green, a sign of life and hope.

The Seven

Symbols of the Sacraments

	Why Do We Celebrate?	Who Is the Ordinary Minister?
Baptism	We are freed from sin, given the gift of God's life (grace), and become members of the Church.	bishop, priest, or deacon
Confirmation	We are sealed with the Gift of the Holy Spirit and are strengthened.	bishop
Eucharist	We are nourished with Christ's own Body and Blood. The Church fulfills the command of Jesus at the Last Supper to "do this in memory of me."	priest or bishop
Penance	We express contrition for our sins, and we are reconciled with God and the Church.	priest or bishop
Anointing of the Sick	The seriously ill and/or the elderly are strengthened and comforted.	priest or bishop
Holy Orders	Baptized men are ordained deacons, priests, and bishops to serve as God's ministers to the Church.	bishop
Matrimony	A baptized man and woman commit themselves to each other and are blessed to carry out the responsibilities of marriage in faithfulness.	man and woman being married

Sacraments

What Do We See?	What Do We Hear?
Pouring of water over forehead or immersion in baptismal pool	"(Name), I baptize you in the name of the Father, and of the Son, and of the Holy Spirit."
Laying on of hand while anointing with Chrism on forehead	"(Name), be sealed with the Gift of the Holy Spirit."
The priest, who through the power of the Holy Spirit, consecrates the bread and wine which become the Body and Blood of Christ. Communicants receiving the Body and Blood of Christ	The priest saying the words of Consecration, "FOR THIS IS MY BODY. . . ." "FOR THIS IS THE CHALICE OF MY BLOOD. . . ." The communicants responding "Amen" to "The Body of Christ" and "The Blood of Christ."
Priest extends right hand or both hands over head of penitent and says words of absolution.	". . . I absolve you from your sins in the name of the Father, and of the Son, and of the Holy Spirit."
Anointing of the sick on their foreheads and hands; laying on of hands on heads of those who are ill	"Through this holy anointing may the Lord in his love and mercy help you with the grace of the Holy Spirit. May the Lord who frees you from sin save you and raise you up."
Laying on of hands; anointing of the hands of newly-ordained priests	(For priests): "Almighty Father, grant this servant of yours the dignity of the priesthood. Renew within him the Spirit of holiness. . . ."
Joining of right hands by the man and woman	"I, (name), take you, [name], to be my wife [husband]. I promise to be true to you in good times and in bad, in sickness and in health. I will love you and honor you all the days of my life."

The Mass

Introductory Rites

Entrance Altar servers, readers, the deacon, and the priest celebrant process forward to the altar. The assembly sings as this takes place. The priest and deacon kiss the altar and bow out of reverence.

Greeting The priest and the assembly make the Sign of the Cross, and the priest reminds us that we are in the presence of Jesus.

Act of Penitence Gathered in God's presence the assembly sees its sinfulness and proclaims the mystery of God's love. We ask for God's mercy in our lives.

Gloria On some Sundays we sing or say this hymn of praise. (page 123)

Collect or Opening Prayer This prayer expresses the theme of the celebration and the hopes and needs of the assembly.

Liturgy of the Word

First Reading This reading is usually from the Old Testament. We hear of God's love and mercy for his people before the time of Christ. We learn of God's covenant with his people and of the ways they lived his law.

Responsorial Psalm We reflect in silence as God's Word enters our hearts. Then we thank God for the Word we just heard.

Second Reading This reading is usually from the New Testament letters, the Acts of the Apostles, or the Book of Revelation. We hear about the first disciples, the teachings of the Apostles, and the beginning of the Church.

Alleluia or Gospel Acclamation We stand to sing the Alleluia or other words of praise. This shows we are ready to share the Good News of Jesus Christ.

Gospel This reading is always from the Gospel of Matthew, Mark, Luke, or John. Proclaimed by the deacon or priest, this reading is about the mission and ministry of Jesus Christ. Jesus' words and actions speak to us today and help us know how to live as his disciples.

Homily The bishop, priest, or deacon talks to us about the readings. His words help us understand what God's Word means to us today. We learn what it means to believe and be members of the Church. We grow closer to God and one another.

Profession of Faith The whole assembly prays together the Nicene Creed (page 121) or the Apostles' Creed (page 121). We are stating aloud what we believe as members of the Church.

Prayer of the Faithful We pray for the needs of all God's people.

Liturgy of the Eucharist

Preparation of the Gifts The altar is prepared by the deacon and the altar servers. We offer gifts. These gifts include the bread and wine and the collection for the Church and for those in need. As members of the assembly carry the bread and wine in a procession to the altar, we sing. The bread and wine are placed on the altar.

Prayer over the Offering The priest asks God to bless and accept our gifts. We respond, "Blessed be God for ever."

Eucharistic Prayer This is the most important prayer of the Church. It is our greatest prayer of praise and thanksgiving. It joins us to Christ and to one another. The beginning of this prayer, the Preface, consists of offering God thanksgiving and praise. We sing together "Holy, Holy, Holy." The rest of the prayer consists of: calling on the Holy Spirit to bless the gifts of bread and wine; the Consecration of the bread and wine, recalling Jesus' words and actions at the Last Supper; recalling Jesus' Passion, Death, Resurrection, and Ascension; remembering that the Eucharist is offered by the Church in Heaven and on earth; praising God and praying a great "Amen" in love of God: Father, Son, and Holy Spirit.

Communion Rite We prepare to receive the Body and Blood of Jesus Christ as spiritual food in Holy Communion.

Lord's Prayer Jesus gave us this prayer that we pray aloud or sing to the Father.

Rite of Peace We pray that Christ's peace be with us always. We offer one another a Sign of Peace to show that we are united in Christ.

Breaking of the Bread We say aloud or sing the Lamb of God, asking Jesus for his mercy, forgiveness, and peace. The priest breaks apart the Host, and we are invited to share in the Eucharist.

Holy Communion Each person receiving Communion is shown the Host and hears "The Body of Christ." Each person is shown the cup and hears "The Blood of Christ." Each person responds "Amen" and receives Holy Communion. While people are receiving Holy Communion, we sing as one. After this we silently reflect on the gift of Jesus that we have just received and of God's presence with us. The priest then prays that the gift of Jesus will help us live as Jesus' disciples.

Concluding Rites

Greeting The priest offers the final prayer. His words serve as a farewell promise that Jesus will be with us all.

Blessing The priest blesses us in the name of the Father, Son, and Holy Spirit. We make the Sign of the Cross as he blesses us.

Dismissal The deacon or priest ends the Mass and sends the assembly forth. The priest and deacon then kiss the altar. They, along with other ministers at the Mass, bow to the altar, and process out as we sing the closing song.

Rites of Penance

The Church has two usual ways to celebrate the Sacrament of Penance and Reconciliation. One way, or rite, is used when an individual meets with the priest for the celebration of the sacrament. The other rite is used when a group gathers to celebrate the sacrament with one or more priests.

Rite for Reconciliation of Individual Penitents

I examine my conscience before meeting with the priest.

Welcoming The priest greets me and I make the Sign of the Cross. The priest asks me to trust in God's mercy.

Reading of the Word of God The priest or I may read something from the Bible.

Confession and Penance I confess my sins. The priest talks to me about loving God and others. He gives me a penance.

Prayer of Penitent and Absolution I pray an Act of Contrition. The priest extends his hand and gives me absolution.

Proclamation of Praise and Dismissal The priest says, "Give thanks to the Lord, for he is good." I respond, "His mercy endures for ever." The priest sends me out saying, "The Lord has freed you from your sins. Go in peace."

Rite for Reconciliation of Several Penitents with Individual Confession and Absolution

Introductory Rites We gather as an assembly and sing an opening hymn. The priest greets us and prays an opening prayer.

Celebration of the Word of God The assembly listens to the Word of God. This is followed by a homily and then by our examination of conscience.

Rite of Reconciliation The assembly prays together an Act of Contrition. We may say another prayer or sing a song, and then pray the Our Father.

I meet individually with the priest and confess my sins. The priest talks to me about loving God and others. He gives me a penance.

The priest extends his hand and gives me absolution.

After everyone has met with the priest, we join together and praise God for his mercy. The priest then offers a prayer of thanksgiving.

Concluding Rite The priest blesses us, and dismisses the assembly saying, "The Lord has freed you from your sins. Go in peace." We respond, "Thanks be to God."

An Examination of Conscience

When we examine our consciences, we can thank God for giving us the strength to make good choices. Reflecting on the choices we have made helps us to make choices that bring us closer to God. Take a few minutes to think quietly and prayerfully about ways you follow each of the commandments. The Ten Commandments state serious obligations to God and our neighbor. The list of commandments is on page 70.

The First Commandment

- Do I try to love God above all things?
- Do I really believe in, trust, and love God?
- Do I pray to God sometime each day?
- How do I take an active part in the worship of God, especially in the Mass and the other sacraments?

The Second Commandment

- Do I respect God's name and the name of Jesus?
- How have I used God's name?
- Have I called on God and asked him to be with me?
- How do I act when I am in church?

The Third Commandment

- How have I kept the Lord's Day holy?
- What do I do to participate in Mass every Sunday?
- On Sundays in what ways have I rested and relaxed? shared time with my family? praised and thanked God?

The Fourth Commandment

- Do I obey my parents, grandparents, or guardians in all that they ask me?
- Do I help them?
- Do I respect my brothers and sisters?
- How have I shown respect for older people?
- Do I obey my teachers and others in authority?
- Have I followed the laws of my city, state, and country?

The Fifth Commandment

- Have I respected the dignity of all people?
- Have I shown by my actions that all people have the right to life?
- Have I done anything that could harm myself or others?
- Have I spoken out against violence and injustice?
- Have I lived in peace with my family and neighbors?

The Sixth Commandment

- Do I honor myself as special and created by God?
- Do my actions show love and respect for myself and others?
- Do I use my body in responsible and faithful ways?

The Seventh Commandment

- Have I cared for the gifts of Creation?
- Have I taken care of my belongings?
- Have I taken things that do not belong to me?
- Have I been honest in taking tests and playing games?
- Have I respected the property of others?
- Have I shared what I have with those in need?

The Eighth Commandment

- Have I taken responsibility for my words and been truthful?
- Have I respected the privacy of others?
- Have I made promises that I did not keep?

The Ninth Commandment

- Do I stay away from things and people who do not live by the virtue of chastity and do not value human sexuality?
- Do I try to show my feelings in a respectful way?
- In what ways do I practice modesty, the virtue by which we think, speak, act, and dress in ways that show respect for ourselves and others?

The Tenth Commandment

- Do I wish that I had things that belong to others?
- Am I sad when others have things that I would like?
- Am I willing to share with others, especially people who are poor and needy?
- Do I give money to the poor and needy?
- Am I happy with what I have or am I always asking for more things?

The Sacrament of Holy Orders

Holy Orders is the sacrament in which baptized men are ordained to serve the Church as deacons, priests, and bishops. It is a Sacrament at the Service of Communion—a sacrament of service to others. While there are many ministries in the Church, deacons, priests, and bishops are the only ordained ministers. Those who receive Holy Orders take on a special mission in leading and serving the People of God.

In the Sacrament of Holy Orders:

Those who receive Holy Orders are forever sealed with a sacramental character. This joins them to Christ and marks them as forever in the service of Christ and the Church. Thus, the Sacrament of Holy Orders cannot be repeated.

Deacons Through Holy Orders, a deacon shares in Christ's mission by assisting bishops and priests in the mission of the Church. Some men, single or married, become permanent deacons, remaining deacons for life.

Other men remain unmarried and become deacons as a step toward the priesthood. Having been ordained as deacons, they continue on to be ordained into the priesthood.

Priests A priest is ordained to preach the Gospel and serve the faithful, especially celebrating the Eucharist and other sacraments.

Bishops To become a bishop, a priest must be chosen by the pope, with the advice of other bishops and Church members. A bishop receives the fullness of the Sacrament of Holy Orders and continues the Apostles' mission of leadership and service.

Ordination In the sacramental act called *ordination*, bishops, priests, and deacons receive one or more of the three degrees of orders: episcopate, (bishops) presbyterate (priests), and diaconate (deacons). A bishop always ordains a newly chosen bishop, as well as candidates for the priesthood and diaconate.

The celebration of Holy Orders always takes place during the Mass. After the bishop celebrant gives a homily, he talks to the men to be ordained, questioning them about their responsibilities to lead and serve in Jesus' name. Then the whole assembly prays for these men.

After the assembly's prayer, the laying on of hands takes place. During the laying on of hands, the bishop celebrant prays in silence. When a priest is ordained, the other priests who are present also lay their hands upon the candidate. This is a sign of their unity in priesthood and service to the diocese. When a bishop is ordained, other bishops lay their hands upon the bishop-elect as a sign of their unity in service to the Church.

After the laying on of hands, the bishop celebrant prays the prayer of consecration, which is different for each degree of orders. The bishop celebrant extends his hands, and by the power of the Holy Spirit ordains each man to continue Jesus' ministry in a particular service in the Church. The laying on of hands and the prayer of consecration are the main parts of the Sacrament of Holy Orders.

The newly ordained men are presented with signs of their service and ministry in the Church. At ordination:

- Deacons receive a stole, which is to be worn across the left shoulder and fastened at the right, a sign of ministry, and the Book of the Gospels, a sign of preaching the Good News of Christ.

- Priests have their stoles placed around the neck and down over the chest; they have the palms of their hands anointed so that they can make the People of God holy through the sacraments. They receive a chalice and a paten, signs that they may celebrate the Eucharist to offer the sacrifice of the Lord.

- Bishops' heads are anointed, and they receive a miter or pointed hat, a sign of the office of bishop; a ring, a sign of faithfulness to Christ and the Church; and a pastor staff, a sign of a bishop's role as shepherd of Christ's flock.

The Sacrament of Matrimony

The Sacrament of Matrimony is the sacrament in which a man and woman become husband and wife, and promise to be faithful to each other for the rest of their lives. It is a Sacrament at the Service of Communion.

The Church sees marriage as a covenant. The marriage covenant is the life-long commitment between a man and a woman to live as faithful and loving partners. It is modeled on Christ's love for the Church, sometimes called the Bride of Christ.

The love that a husband and a wife share with each other is a sign of God's love for all his people. It is a sign of Christ's love for his Church. The love between a husband and wife is meant to be generous, faithful, and complete.

Once Jesus was teaching about marriage, and he said "what God has joined together, no human being must separate" (Matthew 19:6). Thus, Christ and the Church teach us that the marriage covenant is not to be broken. In the Sacrament of Matrimony, the husband and wife promise to be loyal and true to each other for the rest of their lives. If a married couple does have problems in their relationship, they can turn to their family and the parish community for prayer and support. And God's grace continues to help husbands and wives, especially in the Sacraments of the Eucharist and Penance.

The married couple's expression of their love includes the procreation of children, and the education of the children in the faith. With the help of God's grace, married couples are called to create and nurture a loving family, a community of faith, hope, and love.

Every family is called to be a domestic Church, "a Church in the home." It is in the family that we learn to pray and worship God together, to forgive and be forgiven, and to be disciples of Jesus, helping and comforting others, especially those in need.

The celebration of the Sacrament of Matrimony often takes place within the Mass. The Rite of Marriage takes place after the Gospel is proclaimed. The Rite of Marriage begins as the priest or deacon asks the couple three questions. Are they free to give themselves in marriage? Will they love and honor each other as husband and wife throughout their lives? Will they lovingly accept children from God and raise them in the faith?

Then the bride and groom exchange their vows. The deacon or priest asks God to fill the couple's lives with many blessings. Then the deacon or priest blesses the rings, and the couple exchanges them as a sign of their love and faithfulness. After the assembly prays the Prayer of the Faithful, the Mass continues with the Liturgy of the Eucharist. After the Lord's Prayer, the priest prays a special prayer for the couple. The bride and groom, if they are Catholic, receive Holy Communion as a sign of their union with Christ.

Vocations

In Baptism God calls all of us to serve him. A *vocation* is God's call to serve him in a particular way. Each baptized person has a vocation to love and serve God. There are specific ways to follow our vocation: the married or single life, the religious life, or the life of an ordained priest or permanent deacon.

Many Catholics live out their vocation as laypeople in the married life or the single life. Through marriage a husband and wife share God's love in a special way with each other and form a new Christian family. They spend much of their time and energy in loving, caring, and sharing their faith with their families, but can also serve others in their parishes, neighborhoods, and communities. Single people often devote themselves to sharing their gifts and talents with others through their work. They may have more time to dedicate to their parents, families, parishes, and local communities.

Some men and women follow Jesus Christ in the religious life. They are priests, brothers, or sisters who belong to religious communities and make vows, or promises to God. They promise: *poverty*—to live simply as Jesus did, owning no property or personal goods; *chastity*—to live a life of celibacy, remaining single and devoting themselves to the work of God and the Church; *obedience*—to listen carefully to God's direction in their lives by obeying the leaders of the Church and their religious communities.

Some religious live apart from the world spending their days in prayer. Others combine prayer and service in teaching, social work, or the medical field.

God calls some baptized men to be priests and permanent deacons. Priests promise to live a life of celibacy, remaining single. This allows them to serve all of God's people. Diocesan priests serve a diocese, usually in a parish. They serve in the work assigned to them by the bishop. Priests in religious communities serve wherever their communities need them.

Permanent deacons are often married and have an occupation or a career to support themselves and their families. They are ordained to assist the bishops and priests and to serve the whole Church. They preach, baptize, witness marriages, preside at burials, and at Mass they read the Gospel, prepare the altar, and distribute Holy Communion.

Each person can prepare to serve in a particular vocation by praying and reflecting on ways God might be calling him or her to live. See "Prayer for My Vocation" on page 122.

Catholic Social Teaching

Jesus' life and teaching are the foundation of Catholic social teaching. This teaching calls us to work for justice and peace as Jesus did. Catholic social teaching is based on the belief that every person has human dignity. Human dignity is the value and worth that come from being created in God's image and likeness.

There are seven themes of Catholic social teaching.

Life and Dignity of the Human Person Human life is sacred because it is a gift from God. Because we are all God's children, we all share the same human dignity. As Christians we respect all people, even those we do not know.

Call to Family, Community, and Participation We are all social. We need to be with others to grow. The family is the basic community. In the family we grow and learn the values of our faith. As Christians we live those values in our family and community.

Rights and Responsibilities of the Human Person Every person has a fundamental right to life. This includes the things we need to have a decent life: faith and family, work and education, health care and housing. We also have a responsibility to others and to society. We work to make sure the rights of all people are being protected.

Option for the Poor and Vulnerable We have a special obligation to help those who are poor and in need. This includes those who cannot protect themselves because of their age or their health.

Dignity of Work and the Rights of Workers Our work is a sign of our participation in God's work. People have the right to decent work, just wages, safe working conditions, and to participate in decisions about work.

Solidarity of the Human Family Solidarity is a feeling of unity. It binds members of a group together. Each of us is a member of the one human family. The human family includes people of all racial and cultural backgrounds. We all suffer when one part of the human family suffers whether they live near or far away.

Care for God's Creation God created us to be stewards, or caretakers, of his Creation. We must care for and respect the environment. We have to protect it for future generations. When we care for Creation, we show respect for God the Creator.

> Note: The **Corporal Works of Mercy** are found on page 89.
> The **Spiritual Works of Mercy** are found on page 90.

Responding to the Holy Spirit

The Gifts of the Holy Spirit When we are baptized, the Holy Spirit shares seven spiritual gifts with us. These gifts help us to be faithful followers of Jesus Christ. The Gifts of the Holy Spirit are:

- wisdom—helps us to know and be able to follow God's will in our lives

- understanding—helps us to love others as Jesus calls us to do

- counsel (right judgment)—helps us to make good choices

- fortitude (courage)—helps us to be strong in giving witness to our faith in Jesus Christ

- knowledge—helps us to learn more about God and his plan

- piety (reverence)—helps us to have a love and respect for all that God has created

- fear of the Lord (wonder and awe)—helps us to recognize that God's presence and love fills all creation

The Fruits of the Holy Spirit When we respond to the Holy Spirit and use the gifts we have received, the Fruits of the Holy Spirit are evident in our lives. The Fruits of the Holy Spirit are charity, joy, peace, patience, kindness, goodness, generosity, gentleness, faithfulness, modesty, self-control, chastity.

The Precepts of the Church
(from *Catechism of the Catholic Church,* 2041–2043)

1 You shall attend Mass on Sundays and Holy Days of Obligation and rest from servile labor.

2 You shall confess your sins at least once a year.

3 You shall receive the Sacrament of the Eucharist at least during the Easter season.

4 You shall observe the days of fasting and abstinence by the Church.

5 You shall help to provide for the needs of the Church.

About Prayer

Prayer is the raising of our hearts and minds to God. Throughout history—from Creation to the present day—God has called his people to prayer. Prayer is like a conversation: God calls to us, and we respond. Our prayer is a response to God's constant love for us.

We can pray in the silence of our hearts, or we can pray aloud. We can pray alone or with others. Sometimes we do not use words to pray, but sit quietly trying to focus only on God. But however we pray, we turn to God with hope and faith in his love for us.

Jesus taught us to pray by showing us how he prayed. Jesus prayed by quietly focusing on God, studying Scriptures, praying the psalms, giving thanks to his Father, healing people, forgiving people, and talking to God about his feelings. From the example and words of Jesus we learn to pray above all to God the Father. Jesus taught us to do this most especially in the Lord's Prayer.

The Lord's Prayer

The Lord's Prayer, also called the Our Father, "is truly the summary of the whole gospel" (*Catechism of the Catholic Church*, 2761). It sums up Jesus' message of trust in and love for the Father.

When we pray the Lord's Prayer, we are asking our Father to act in our lives and in our world so that we do what he wills. We ask the Holy Spirit to help us to make the Kingdom of God come alive in people's hearts and lives. And we hope for the Lord's return at the end of time.

Praying Always

The Holy Spirit guides the Church to pray. Saint Paul wrote to the early Christian communities, "Pray without ceasing" (1 Thessalonians 5:17). We do this, too, calling on God throughout the day, remembering his presence among us.

The habit of daily prayer grows by making special times for personal prayer:

- in the morning, offering our entire day to God

- before and after meals, giving God thanks for our food

- at night, reflecting on ways we have or have not shown love for God and others.

The habit of daily prayer also grows by joining in prayer with other members of the Church. We do this when we gather with our parish for the celebration of the Mass. Another way is through the Liturgy of the Hours. The Liturgy of the Hours is made up of psalms, readings from Scripture and Church teaching, prayers and hymns. It is celebrated at various times during the day, and helps us to praise God throughout the entire day. Praying the Liturgy of the Hours reminds us that God is always active and present in our lives.

Forms of Prayer

Urged by the Holy Spirit, we pray these basic forms of prayer.

Prayers of blessing

"The grace of the Lord Jesus Christ and the love of God and the fellowship of the holy Spirit be with all of you."
(2 Corinthians 13:13)

To bless is to dedicate someone or something to God or to make something holy in God's name. God continually blesses us with many gifts. Because God first blessed us, we, too, can pray for his blessings on people and things.

Prayers of petition

"O God, be merciful to me a sinner."
(Luke 18:13)

In prayers of petition we ask something of God. Asking for forgiveness is the most important type of petition.

Prayers of intercession

"And this is my prayer: that your love may increase ever more and more in knowledge." (Philippians 1:9)

Intercession is a type of petition. When we pray a prayer of intercession, we are asking for something on behalf of another person or a group of people.

Prayers of thanksgiving

"Father, I thank you for hearing me."
(John 11:41)

In prayers of thanksgiving, we show our gratitude to God for all he has given to us, most especially for the life, Death, and Resurrection of Jesus. The greatest prayer of thanksgiving is the greatest prayer of the Church, the Eucharist.

Prayers of praise

"I shall praise the LORD all my life, sing praise to my God while I live."
(Psalm 146:2)

In prayers of praise we give glory to God for being God. We praise God simply because he is God.

Prayers and Practices

Do you know about sacramentals?

Blessings, actions, and objects that help us respond to God's grace received in the sacraments are *sacramentals*. Sacramentals are used in the liturgy and in personal prayer. Here are some examples of sacramentals:

- blessings of people, places, foods, and objects
- objects such as rosaries, medals, crucifixes, blessed ashes, and blessed palms
- actions such as making the Sign of the Cross and sprinkling holy water.

The Rosary

The rosary is a sacramental. Praying the rosary is a popular devotion to Mary. We can pray the rosary alone or with others. We can pray the rosary at any time of the day.

The rosary is usually prayed using a set of beads with a crucifix attached. We repeatedly pray the Our Father, Hail Mary, and Glory to the Father on these beads. This creates a peaceful rhythm of prayer during which we can reflect on special events in the lives of Jesus and Mary. The mysteries of the rosary recall these special events. We remember a different mystery at the beginning of each set of prayers, or decade of the rosary.

Mysteries of the Rosary

The Joyful Mysteries
(by custom prayed on Monday and Saturday)
- The Annunciation
- The Visitation
- The Birth of Jesus
- The Presentation of Jesus in the Temple
- The Finding of Jesus in the Temple

The Sorrowful Mysteries
(by custom prayed on Tuesday and Friday)
- The Agony in the Garden
- The Scourging at the Pillar
- The Crowning with Thorns
- The Carrying of the Cross
- The Crucifixion and Death of Jesus

The Glorious Mysteries
(by custom prayed on Wednesday and Sunday)
- The Resurrection
- The Ascension
- The Descent of the Holy Spirit upon the Apostles
- The Assumption of Mary into Heaven
- The Coronation of Mary as Queen of Heaven

The Mysteries of Light
(by custom prayed on Thursday)
- Jesus' Baptism in the Jordan
- The Miracle at the Wedding at Cana
- Jesus Announces the Kingdom of God
- The Transfiguration
- The Institution of the Eucharist

Prayers of the Rosary

1. Sign of the Cross (see page 10)
2. Apostles' Creed (see page 121)
3. Our Father (see page 17)
4. Hail Mary (see page 97)
5. Glory to the Father (see page 11)
6. Hail, Holy Queen (see right column)

Hail, Holy Queen

Hail, holy Queen, mother of mercy,
hail, our life, our sweetness, and our hope.
To you we cry, the children of Eve;
to you we send up our sighs,
mourning and weeping in this land of exile.
Turn, then, most gracious advocate,
your eyes of mercy toward us;
lead us home at last
and show us the blessed fruit of your
    womb, Jesus:
O clement, O loving, O sweet Virgin Mary.

6. Pray the Hail, Holy Queen to end the rosary.

5. Pray a Glory to the Father after each set of small beads.

4. Pray the Hail Mary at every small bead.

3. Pray an Our Father at every large bead.

2. Pray the Apostles' Creed.

1. Start with the Sign of the Cross.

Note: Follow 1 to 6 to pray the rosary. See the correlating numbers above to find the words for each prayer.

Visit the Most Blessed Sacrament

After Communion at Mass, the consecrated Hosts that remain are placed in the tabernacle. This reserved Eucharist is called the Most Blessed Sacrament. A special light, called the *sanctuary lamp*, is always kept burning nearby. This light reminds us that Jesus Christ is truly present in the Most Blessed Sacrament. We can "make a visit to Jesus" in the Most Blessed Sacrament. Our prayer shows Jesus our love for him. It continues the thanksgiving that was begun at Mass.

Benediction

Benediction is a very old practice in the Church. The word *benediction* comes from a Latin word for "blessing."

At Benediction a large Host that was consecrated during Mass is placed in a special holder called a *monstrance,* (comes from a Latin word meaning "to show") so that all can see the Most Blessed Sacrament. Benediction includes hymns, a blessing, and praying the "Divine Praises."

Divine Praises

Blessed be God.
Blessed be his holy name.
Blessed be Jesus Christ, true God and true man.
Blessed be the name of Jesus.
Blessed be his most sacred heart.
Blessed be his most precious blood.
Blessed be Jesus in the most holy sacrament of the altar.
Blessed be the Holy Spirit, the Paraclete.
Blessed be the great mother of God, Mary most holy.
Blessed be her holy and immaculate conception.
Blessed be her glorious assumption.
Blessed be the name of Mary, virgin and mother.
Blessed be Saint Joseph, her most chaste spouse.
Blessed be God in his angels and in his saints.

Processions

Many parishes have processions on special feast days. Often the priest leads the procession carrying the Blessed Sacrament in a monstrance. Benediction of the Blessed Sacrament often takes place at the end of the procession.

Pilgrimages

Some people make pilgrimages, or prayer journeys, to holy places or shrines to honor Mary and the saints.

Nicene Creed

I believe in one God,
the Father almighty,
maker of heaven and earth,
of all things visible and invisible.

I believe in one Lord Jesus Christ,
the Only Begotten Son of God,
born of the Father before all ages.
God from God, Light from Light,
true God from true God,
begotten, not made, consubstantial
with the Father;
through him all things were made.
For us men and for our salvation
he came down from heaven,
and by the Holy Spirit
was incarnate of the Virgin Mary,
and became man.

For our sake he was crucified
under Pontius Pilate,
he suffered death and was buried,
and rose again on the third day
in accordance with the Scriptures.
He ascended into heaven
and is seated at the right hand
of the Father.
He will come again in glory
to judge the living and the dead
and his kingdom will have no end.

I believe in the Holy Spirit, the Lord,
the giver of life,
who proceeds from the Father
and the Son,
who with the Father and the Son is
adored and glorified,
who has spoken through the prophets.
I believe in one, holy, catholic
and apostolic Church.
I confess one Baptism
for the forgiveness of sins
and I look forward to the resurrection of the dead
and the life of the world to come.
Amen.

Apostles' Creed

I believe in God, the Father almighty,
Creator of heaven and earth,
and in Jesus Christ, his only Son, our Lord,
who was conceived by the Holy Spirit,
born of the Virgin Mary,
suffered under Pontius Pilate,
was crucified, died and was buried;
he descended into hell;
on the third day he rose again
from the dead;
he ascended into heaven,
and is seated at the right hand
of God the Father almighty;
from there he will come to judge
the living and the dead.

I believe in the Holy Spirit,
the holy catholic Church,
the communion of saints,
the forgiveness of sins,
the resurrection of the body,
and life everlasting. Amen.

Note: The Sign of the Cross is on page 10.
Glory to the Father is on page 11.
The Lord's Prayer, is on page 17.
Come, Holy Spirit is on page 31.
Act of Contrition is on page 85.
Hail Mary is on page 97.
Hail, Holy Queen is on page 119.

Morning Offering

O Jesus, I offer you all my prayers,
    works and suffering of this day
for all the intentions of your most
    Sacred Heart.
Amen.

Evening Prayer

Dear God, before I sleep
I want to thank you for this day,
so full of your kindness and your joy.
I close my eyes to rest
safe in your loving care.

Grace Before Meals

Bless us, O Lord, and these your gifts
which we are about to receive from
    your goodness.
Through Christ our Lord.
Amen.

Prayer After Meals

We give you thanks for all your gifts,
    almighty God,
living and reigning now and for ever.
Amen.

Prayer for My Vocation

Dear God,
you have a great and loving plan
for our world and for me.
I wish to share in that plan fully,
faithfully, and joyfully.

Help me to understand what it is
you wish me to do in my life.
Help me to be attentive to the signs
that you give me about preparing
    for the future.

Help me to learn to be a sign of the Kingdom
of God, whether I am called to the priesthood
or religious life, the single or married life.

And once I have heard and understood
your call, give me the strength
and the grace to follow it
with generosity and love. Amen.

Prayer for My Discipleship

Jesus, you invite me to be your disciple.
You showed me how to love God the Father
with all my heart, with all my soul, and with
    all my mind.
You showed me how to love my neighbors
and the importance of loving myself.

It is not always easy to be a disciple.
I am grateful for the example you have
    given to me.
Jesus, continue to guide me
and strengthen me on my journey
    to be your disciple. Amen.

Prayers from the Celebration of the Eucharist

Confiteor

I confess to almighty God
and to you, my brothers and sisters,
that I have greatly sinned,
in my thoughts and in my words,
in what I have done and in what I have failed to do,
through my fault, through my fault,
through my most grievous fault;
therefore I ask blessed Mary ever-Virgin,
all the Angels and Saints,
and you, my brothers and sisters,
to pray for me to the Lord our God. Amen.

Gloria

Glory to God in the highest,
and on earth peace to people of good will.

We praise you,
we bless you,
we adore you,
we glorify you,
we give you thanks for your great glory,
Lord God, heavenly King,
O God, almighty Father.

Lord Jesus Christ, Only Begotten Son,
Lord God, Lamb of God, Son of the Father,
you take away the sins of the world,
    have mercy on us;
you take away the sins of the world,
    receive our prayer;
you are seated at the right hand of the Father,
    have mercy on us.

For you alone are the Holy One,
you alone are the Lord,
you alone are the Most High,
Jesus Christ,
with the Holy Spirit,
in the glory of God the Father. Amen.

Lamb of God

Lamb of God, you take away the
        sins of the world,
    have mercy on us.
Lamb of God, you take away the
        sins of the world,
    have mercy on us.
Lamb of God, you take away the
        sins of the world,
    grant us peace.

Prayer After Communion

(These words may be prayed quietly after you receive Holy Communion.)

Jesus,
thank you for coming to me in
        Communion.
Thank you for strengthening me
    to be your disciple and to serve others.
Help me to be grateful for each day
    and to stay close to you always.
Amen.

Note: The Nicene Creed is on on page 121.
Holy, Holy, Holy is on page 65.
Memorial Acclamations are on page 23.

Glossary

absolution (page 83) forgiveness of our sins by the priest in the name of Christ and the Church and through the power of the Holy Spirit in the Sacrament of Penance and Reconciliation

Annunciation (page 95) the announcement to Mary that she would be the Mother of the Son of God

Apostles (page 15) the twelve men whom Jesus chose to share in his mission in a special way

Ascension (page 28) Jesus' return in all his glory to his Father in Heaven

assembly (page 62) the community of people who gather for the celebration of the Mass

Assumption (page 95) the truth that when Mary's work on earth was done, God brought Mary body and soul to live forever with the risen Christ

Baptism (page 50) the sacrament in which we are freed from sin, become children of God, and are welcomed into the Church

Beatitudes (page 77) Jesus' teachings that describe the way to live as his disciples

Bible (page 8) the book about God's love for us and about our call to live as God's people: the Bible is the Word of God.

bishops (page 34) men who have received the fullness of the Sacrament of Holy Orders, and as the successors of the Apostles continue to lead the Church

Blessed Trinity (page 10) the three Persons in one God: God the Father, God the Son, and God the Holy Spirit

celebrant (page 51) the bishop, priest, or deacon who celebrates a sacrament for and with the community

charity (page 78) or love, the greatest of all virtues that enables us to love God and to love our neighbor

Chrism (page 51) perfumed oil blessed by the bishop

Church (page 29) the community of people who are baptized and follow Jesus Christ

Communion of Saints (page 94) the union of the baptized members of the Church on earth with those who are in Heaven and in Purgatory

Concluding Rites (page 64) the last part of the Mass in which we are sent to love and serve the Lord each day by bringing the peace and love of Jesus to everyone we meet

confession (page 83) telling our sins to the priest in the Sacrament of Penance and Reconciliation

Confirmation (page 52) the sacrament in which we receive the Gift of the Holy Spirit in a special way

conscience (page 83) our ability to know the difference between good and evil, right and wrong

contrition (page 83) being sorry for our sins and promising not to sin again

conversion (page 82) turning back to God with all one's heart

Corporal Works of Mercy (page 89) acts of love that help us care for the physical and material needs of others

covenant (page 70) a special agreement between God and his people

deacon (page 36) a baptized man who in the Sacrament of Holy Orders, has been ordained to serve the Church by preaching, baptizing, performing marriages, and doing acts of charity

diocese (page 34) local areas of the Church, each led by a bishop

disciples (page 15) those who follow Jesus

divine (page 14) a word we use to describe God

Eucharist (page 56) the sacrament of the Body and Blood of Christ, Jesus is truly present to us under the appearances of bread and wine

faith (page 78) the virtue that enables us to believe in God and all that the Church teaches us

grace (page 41) the gift of God's life in us

hope (page 78) the virtue that enables us to trust in God's promise to share his life with us forever

Immaculate Conception (page 95) the truth that God created Mary free from Original Sin and from all sin from the very first moment of her life, her conception

Incarnation (page 14) the truth that God the Son, the second Person of the Blessed Trinity, became man

Introductory Rites (page 62) the part of the Mass that unites us as a community, prepares us to hear God's Word, and to celebrate the Eucharist

Kingdom of God (page 16) the power of God's love active in our lives and in our world

Last Supper (page 20) the last meal Jesus shared with his disciples before he died

Liturgy of the Eucharist (page 63) the part of the Mass when the bread and wine become the Body and Blood of Christ

Liturgy of the Word (page 62) the part of the Mass when we listen and respond to God's Word

Marks of the Church (page 35) the four characteristics of the Church: one, holy, catholic, and apostolic

Original Sin (page 9) the first sin committed by the first human beings

parish (page 36) a community of believers who gather together to worship God and work together

pastor (page 36) the priest who leads the parish in worship, prayer, teaching, and service

penance (page 83) a prayer or an act of service that we do to show we are sorry for our sins

Pentecost (page 29) the day the Holy Spirit came upon Jesus' disciples

pope (page 34) the Bishop of Rome who leads and guides the Catholic Church

priests (page 36) baptized men who are ordained to preach the Gospel and serve the faithful, especially by celebrating the Eucharist and the other sacraments

Real Presence (page 20) the true presence of Jesus Christ in the Eucharist

Resurrection (page 22) the mystery of Jesus Christ rising from the dead

sacrament (page 41) an effective sign given to us by Jesus Christ through which we share in God's life

sacrifice (page 57) a gift offered to God by a priest in the name of all the people

saints (page 94) followers of Christ who lived lives of holiness on earth and now share in eternal life with God in Heaven

Savior (page 22) a title given to Jesus because he died and rose from the dead to save us

sin (page 83) a thought, word, deed, or omission against God's law

Spiritual Works of Mercy (page 90) acts of love that help us care for the needs of people's hearts, minds, and souls

Ten Commandments (page 70) the laws of God's covenant given to Moses for all the people

virtue (page 78) a good habit that helps us to act according to God's love for us

Works of Mercy (page 89) the loving acts that we do to care for the needs of others

Index